A Bit O' Love by John Galsworthy

Fourth Series Plays

John Galsworthy was born at Kingston Upon Thames in Surrey, England, on August 14th 1867 to a wealthy and well established family. His schooling was at Harrow and New College, Oxford before training as a barrister and being called to the bar in 1890. However, Law was not attractive to him and he travelled abroad becoming great friends with the novelist Joseph Conrad, then a first mate on a sailing ship.

In 1895 Galsworthy began an affair with Ada Nemesis Pearson Cooper, the wife of his cousin Major Arthur Galsworthy. The affair was kept a secret for 10 years till she at last divorced and they married on 23 September 1905.

John Galsworthy first published in 1897 with a collection of short stories entitled "The Four Winds". For the next 7 years he published these and all works under his pen name John Sinjohn. It was only upon the death of his father and the publication of "The Island Pharisees" in 1904 that he published as John Galsworthy. In this volume we have Villa Rubein ays and studies. They are the work of a supreme talent at the top of his game. Whilst today he is far more well know as a Nobel Prize winning novelist then he was considered a playwright dealing with social issues and the class system. He was appointed to the Order of Merit in 1929, after earlier turning down a knighthood, and awarded the Nobel Prize in 1932 though he was too ill to attend. John Galsworthy died from a brain tumour at his London home, Grove Lodge, Hampstead on January 31st 1933. In accordance with his will he was cremated at Woking with his ashes then being scattered over the South Downs from an aeroplane.

He is now far better known for his novels, particularly The Forsyte Saga, his trilogy about the eponymous family of the same name. These books, as with many of his other works, deal with social class, upper-middle class lives in particular. Although always sympathetic to his characters, he reveals their insular, snobbish, and somewhat greedy attitudes and suffocating moral codes. He is now viewed as one of the first from the Edwardian era to challenge some of the ideals of society depicted in the literature of Victorian England.

In his writings he campaigns for a variety of causes, including prison reform, women's rights, animal welfare, and the opposition of censorship as well as a recurring theme of an unhappy marriage from the women's side. During World War I he worked in a hospital in France as an orderly after being passed over for military service.

He was appointed to the Order of Merit in 1929, after earlier turning down a knighthood, and awarded the Nobel Prize in 1932 though he was too ill to attend.

John Galsworthy died from a brain tumour at his London home, Grove Lodge, Hampstead on January 31st 1933. In accordance with his will he was cremated at Woking with his ashes then being scattered over the South Downs from an aeroplane.

Index of Contents

PERSONS OF THE PLAY
SCENE - A VILLAGE OF THE WEST
TIME - The Action passes on Ascension Day.
ACT I - Strangway's rooms at Burlacombe's. Morning.
ACT II - Evening
SCENE I - The Village Inn.
SCENE II - The same.
SCENE III - Outside the church.
ACT III - Evening
SCENE I - STRANGWAY'S rooms.
SCENE II - BURLACOMBE'S barn.
JOHN GALSWORTHY – A SHORT BIOGRAPHY
JOHN GALSWORTHY – A CONCISE BIBLIOGRAPHY

PERSONS OF THE PLAY
MICHAEL STRANGWAY
BEATRICE STRANGWAY
MRS BRADMERE
JIM BERE
JACK CREMER
MRS BURLACOMBE
BURLACOMBE
TRUSTAFORD
JARLAND
CLYST
FREMAN
GODLEIGH
SOL POTTER
MORSE, AND OTHERS
IVY BURLACOMBE
CONNIE TRUSTAFORD
GLADYS FREMAN
MERCY JARLAND
TIBBY JARLAND
BOBBIE JARLAND

A BIT O' LOVE

ACT I

It is Ascension Day in a village of the West. In the low panelled hall-sittingroom of the Burlacombe's farmhouse on the village green, **MICHAEL STRANGWAY**, a clerical collar round his throat and a dark Norfolk jacket on his back, is playing the flute before a very large framed photograph of a woman, which is the only picture on the walls. His age is about thirty-five his figure thin and very upright and his clean-shorn face thin, upright, narrow, with long and rather pointed ears; his dark hair is brushed in a coxcomb off his forehead. A faint smile hovers about his lips that Nature has made rather full and he has made thin, as though keeping a hard secret; but his bright grey eyes, dark round the rim, look out and upwards almost as if he were being crucified. There is something about the whole of him that makes him seen not quite present. A gentle creature, burnt within.

A low broad window above a window-seat forms the background to his figure; and through its lattice panes are seen the outer gate and yew-trees of a churchyard and the porch of a church, bathed in May sunlight. The front door at right angles to the window-seat, leads to the village green, and a door on the left into the house.

It is the third movement of Veracini's violin sonata that **STRANGWAY** plays. His back is turned to the door into the house, and he does not hear when it is opened, and **IVY BURLACOMBE**, the farmer's daughter, a girl of fourteen, small and quiet as a mouse, comes in, a prayer-book in one hand, and in the other a glass of water, with wild orchids and a bit of deep pink hawthorn. She sits down on the window-seat, and having opened her book, sniffs at the flowers. Coming to the end of the movement **STRANGWAY** stops, and looking up at the face on the wall, heaves a long sigh.

IVY [From the seat]
I picked these for yu, Mr. Strangway.

STRANGWAY [Turning with a start]
Ah! Ivy. Thank you.

[He puts his flute down on a chair against the far wall]

Where are the others?

[As he speaks, **GLADYS FREMAN**, a dark gipsyish girl, and **CONNIE TRUSTAFORD**, a fair, stolid, blue-eyed Saxon, both about sixteen, come in through the front door, behind which they have evidently been listening. They too have prayer-books in their hands. They sidle past **IVY**, and also sit down under the window.

GLADYS
Mercy's comin', Mr. Strangway.

STRANGWAY
Good morning, Gladys; good morning, Connie.

[He turns to a book-case on a table against the far wall, and taking out a book, finds his place in it. While he stands thus with his back to the girls, **MERCY JARLAND** comes in from the green. She also is about sixteen, with fair hair and china-blue eyes. She glides in quickly, hiding something behind her, and sits down on the seat next the door. And at once there is a whispering.

STRANGWAY [Turning to them]
Good morning, Mercy.

MERCY

Good morning, Mr. Strangway.

STRANGWAY
Now, yesterday I was telling you what our Lord's coming meant to the world. I want you to understand that before He came there wasn't really love, as we know it. I don't mean to say that there weren't many good people; but there wasn't love for the sake of loving. D'you think you understand what I mean?

[**MERCY** fidgets. **GLADYS'S** eyes are following a fly.

IVY
Yes, Mr. Strangway.

STRANGWAY
It isn't enough to love people because they're good to you, or because in some way or other you're going to get something by it. We have to love because we love loving. That's the great thing —without that we're nothing but Pagans.

GLADYS
Please, what is Pagans?

STRANGWAY
That's what the first Christians called the people who lived in the villages and were not yet Christians, Gladys.

MERCY
We live in a village, but we're Christians.

STRANGWAY [With a smile]
Yes, Mercy; and what is a Christian?

[**MERCY** kicks afoot, sideways against her neighbour, frowns over her china-blare eyes, is silent; then, as his question passes on, makes a quick little face, wriggles, and looks behind her.

STRANGWAY
Ivy?

IVY
'Tis a man—whu—whu—

STRANGWAY
Yes?—Connie?

CONNIE [Who speaks rather thickly, as if she had a permanent slight cold]
Please, Mr. Strangway, 'tis a man what goes to church.

GLADYS
He 'as to be baptised—and confirmed; and—and—buried.

IVY
'Tis a man whu—whu's gude and—

GLADYS
He don't drink, an' he don't beat his horses, an' he don't
hit back.

MERCY [Whispering]
'Tisn't your turn. [To **STRANGWAY**] 'Tis a man like us.

IVY
I know what Mrs. Strangway said it was, 'cause I asked her once, before she went away.

STRANGWAY [Startled]
Yes?

IVY
She said it was a man whu forgave everything.

STRANGWAY
Ah!

[The note of a cuckoo comes travelling. The girls are gazing at **STRANGWAY**, who seems to have gone off into a dream. They begin to fidget and whisper.

CONNIE
Please, Mr. Strangway, father says if yu hit a man and he don't hit yu back, he's no gude at all.

MERCY
When Tommy Morse wouldn't fight, us pinched him—he did squeal! [She giggles] Made me laugh!

STRANGWAY
Did I ever tell you about St. Francis of Assisi?

IVY [Clasping her hands]
No.

STRANGWAY
Well, he was the best Christian, I think, that ever lived—simply full of love and joy.

IVY
I expect he's dead.

STRANGWAY
About seven hundred years, Ivy.

IVY [Softly]

Oh!

STRANGWAY
Everything to him was brother or sister—the sun and the moon, and all that was poor and weak and sad, and animals and birds, so that they even used to follow him about.

MERCY
I know! He had crumbs in his pocket.

STRANGWAY
No; he had love in his eyes.

IVY
'Tis like about Orpheus, that yu told us.

STRANGWAY
Ah! But St. Francis was a Christian, and Orpheus was a Pagan.

IVY
Oh!

STRANGWAY
Orpheus drew everything after him with music; St. Francis by love.

IVY
Perhaps it was the same, really.

STRANGWAY [looking at his flute]
Perhaps it was, Ivy.

GLADYS
Did 'e 'ave a flute like yu?

IVY
The flowers smell sweeter when they 'ear music; they du.

[She holds up the glass of flowers.]

STRANGWAY [Touching one of the orchids]
What's the name of this one?

[The girls cluster; save **MERCY**, who is taking a stealthy interest in what she has behind her.]

CONNIE
We call it a cuckoo, Mr. Strangway.

GLADYS

'Tis awful common down by the streams. We've got one medder where 'tis so thick almost as the goldie cups.

STRANGWAY
Odd! I've never noticed it.

IVY
Please, Mr. Strangway, yu don't notice when yu're walkin'; yu go along like this.

[She holds up her face as one looking at the sky.]

STRANGWAY
Bad as that, Ivy?

IVY
Mrs. Strangway often used to pick it last spring.

STRANGWAY
Did she? Did she?

[He has gone off again into a kind of dream.]

MERCY
I like being confirmed.

STRANGWAY
Ah! Yes. Now—What's that behind you, Mercy?

MERCY [Engagingly producing a cage a little bigger than a mouse-trap, containing a skylark]
My skylark.

STRANGWAY
What!

MERCY
It can fly; but we're goin' to clip its wings. Bobbie caught it.

STRANGWAY
How long ago?

MERCY
[Conscious of impending disaster] Yesterday.

STRANGWAY [White hot]
Give me the cage!

MERCY [Puckering]
I want my skylark.

[As he steps up to her and takes the cage—thoroughly alarmed]

I gave Bobbie thrippence for it!

STRANGWAY [Producing a sixpence]
There!

MERCY [Throwing it down-passionately]
I want my skylark!

STRANGWAY
God made this poor bird for the sky and the grass. And you put it in that! Never cage any wild thing! Never!

MERCY [Faint and sullen]
I want my skylark.

STRANGWAY [Taking the cage to the door]
No!

[He holds up the cage and opens it]

Off you go, poor thing!

[The bird flies out and away. The girls watch with round eyes the fling up of his arm, and the freed bird flying away.]

IVY
I'm glad!

[**MERCY** kicks her viciously and sobs. **STRANGWAY** comes from the door, looks at **MERCY** sobbing, and suddenly clasps his head. The girls watch him with a queer mixture of wonder, alarm, and disapproval.]

GLADYS [Whispering]
Don't cry, Mercy. Bobbie'll soon catch yu another.

[**STRANGWAY** has dropped his hands, and is looking again at **MERCY**. **IVY** sits with hands clasped, gazing at **STRANGWAY**. **MERCY** continues her artificial sobbing.]

STRANGWAY [Quietly]
The class is over for to-day.

[He goes up to **MERCY**, and holds out his hand. She does not take it, and runs out knuckling her eyes. **STRANGWAY** turns on his heel and goes into the house.]

CONNIE
'Twasn't his bird.

IVY

Skylarks belong to the sky. Mr. Strangway said so.

GLADYS

Not when they'm caught, they don't.

IVY

They du.

CONNIE

'Twas her bird.

IVY

He gave her sixpence for it.

GLADYS

She didn't take it.

CONNIE

There it is on the ground.

IVY

She might have.

GLADYS

He'll p'raps take my squirrel, tu.

IVY

The bird sang—I 'eard it! Right up in the sky. It wouldn't have sanged if it weren't glad.

GLADYS

Well, Mercy cried.

IVY

I don't care.

GLADYS

'Tis a shame! And I know something. Mrs. Strangway's at Durford.

CONNIE

She's—never!

GLADYS

I saw her yesterday. An' if she's there she ought to be here. I told mother, an' she said: "Yu mind yer business." An' when she goes in to market to-morrow she'm goin' to see. An' if she's really there, mother says, 'tis a fine tu-du an' a praaper scandal. So I know a lot more'n yu du.

[**IVY** stares at her.]

CONNIE
Mrs. Strangway told mother she was goin' to France for the winter because her mother was ill.

GLADYS
'Tisn't, winter now—Ascension Day. I saw her cumin' out o' Dr. Desert's house. I know 'twas her because she had on a blue dress an' a proud luke. Mother says the doctor come over here tu often before Mrs. Strangway went away, just afore Christmas. They was old sweethearts before she married Mr. Strangway. [To **IVY**] 'Twas yure mother told mother that.

[**IVY** gazes at them more and more wide-eyed.]

CONNIE
Father says if Mrs. Bradmere an' the old Rector knew about the doctor, they wouldn't 'ave Mr. Strangway 'ere for curate any longer; because mother says it takes more'n a year for a gude wife to leave her 'usband, an' 'e so fond of her. But 'tisn't no business of ours, father says.

GLADYS
Mother says so tu. She's praaper set against gossip. She'll know all about it to-morrow after market.

IVY [Stamping her foot]
I don't want to 'ear nothin' at all; I don't, an' I won't.

[A rather shame faced silence falls on the girls.]

GLADYS [In a quick whisper]
'Ere's Mrs. Burlacombe.

[There enters fawn the house a stout motherly woman with a round grey eye and very red cheeks.]

MRS BURLACOMBE
Ivy, take Mr. Strangway his ink, or we'll never 'eve no sermon to-night. He'm in his thinkin' box, but 'tis not a bit o' yuse 'im thinkin' without 'is ink.

[She hands her daughter an inkpot and blotting-pad. **IVY** takes them and goes out]

What ever's this?

[She picks up the little bird-cage.]

GLADYS
'Tis Mercy Jarland's. Mr. Strangway let her skylark go.

MRS BURLACOMBE
Aw! Did 'e now? Serve 'er right, bringin' an 'eathen bird to confirmation class.

CONNIE

I'll take it to her.

MRS BURLACOMBE

No. Yu leave it there, an' let Mr. Strangway du what 'e likes with it. Bringin' a bird like that! Well 'I never!

[The **GIRLS**, perceiving that they have lighted on stony soil, look at each other and slide towards the door.]

MRS BURLACOMBE

Yes, yu just be off, an' think on what yu've been told in class, an' be'ave like Christians, that's gude maids. An' don't yu come no more in the 'avenin's dancin' them 'eathen dances in my barn, naighther, till after yu'm confirmed—'tisn't right. I've told Ivy I won't 'ave it.

CONNIE

Mr. Strangway don't mind—he likes us to; 'twas Mrs. Strangway began teachin' us. He's goin' to give a prize.

MRS BURLACOMBE

Yu just du what I tell yu an' never mind Mr. Strangway—he'm tu kind to everyone. D'yu think I don't know how gells oughter be'ave before confirmation? Yu be'ave like I did! Now, goo ahn! Shoo!

[She hustles them out, rather as she might hustle her chickens, and begins tidying the room. There comes a wandering figure to the open window. It is that of a man of about thirty-five, of feeble gait, leaning the weight of all one side of him on a stick. His dark face, with black hair, one lock of which has gone white, was evidently once that of an ardent man. Now it is slack, weakly smiling, and the brown eyes are lost, and seem always to be asking something to which there is no answer.]

MRS BURLACOMBE [With that forced cheerfulness always assumed in the face of too great misfortune] Well, Jim! better?

[At the faint brightening of the smile]

That's right! Yu'm gettin' on bravely. Want Parson?

JIM [Nodding and smiling, and speaking slowly]
I want to tell 'un about my cat.

[His face loses its smile.]

MRS BURLACOMBE

Why! what's she been duin' then? Mr. Strangway's busy. Won't I du?

JIM [Shaking his head]
No. I want to tell him.

MRS BURLACOMBE

Whatever she been duin'? Havin' kittens?

JIM
No. She'm lost.

MRS BURLACOMBE
Dearie me! Aw! she'm not lost. Cats be like maids; they must get out a bit.

JIM
She'm lost. Maybe he'll know where she'll be.

MRS BURLACOMBE
Well, well. I'll go an' find 'im.

JIM
He's a gude man. He's very gude.

MRS BURLACOMBE
That's certain zure.

STRANGWAY [Entering from the house]
Mrs. Burlacombe, I can't think where I've put my book on St. Francis—the large, squarish pale-blue one?

MRS BURLACOMBE
Aw! there now! I knu there was somethin' on me mind. Miss Willis she came in yesterday afternune when yu was out, to borrow it. Oh! yes—I said—I'm zure Mr. Strangway'll lend it 'ee. Now think o' that!

STRANGWAY
Of course, Mrs. Burlacombe; very glad she's got it.

MRS BURLACOMBE
Aw! but that's not all. When I tuk it up there come out a whole flutter o' little bits o' paper wi' little rhymes on 'em, same as I see yu writin'. Aw! my gudeness! I says to meself, Mr. Strangway widn' want no one seein' them.

STRANGWAY
Dear me! No; certainly not!

MRS BURLACOMBE
An' so I putt 'em in your secretary.

STRANGWAY
My-ah! Yes. Thank you; yes.

MRS BURLACOMBE
But I'll goo over an' get the buke for yu.
'T won't take me 'alf a minit.

[She goes out on to the green. **JIM BERE** has come in.]

STRANGWAY [Gently]
Well, Jim?

JIM
My cat's lost.

STRANGWAY
Lost?

JIM
Day before yesterday. She'm not come back. They've shot 'er, I think; or she'm caught in one o' they rabbit-traps.

STRANGWAY
Oh! no; my dear fellow, she'll come back. I'll speak to Sir Herbert's keepers.

JIM
Yes, zurr. I feel lonesome without 'er.

STRANGWAY [With a faint smile—more to himself than to **JIM**]
Lonesome! Yes! That's bad, Jim! That's bad!

JIM
I miss 'er when I sits than in the avenin'.

STRANGWAY
The evenings—They're the worst—and when the blackbirds sing in the morning.

JIM
She used to lie on my bed, ye know, zurr.

[**STRANGWAY** turns his face away, contracted with pain]

She'm like a Christian.

STRANGWAY
The beasts are.

JIM
There's plenty folk ain't 'alf as Christian as 'er be.

STRANGWAY
Well, dear Jim, I'll do my very best. And any time you're lonely, come up, and I'll play the flute to you.

JIM [Wriggling slightly]
No, zurr. Thank 'ee, zurr.

STRANGWAY
What—don't you like music?

JIM
Ye-es, zurr.

[A figure passes the window. Seeing it he says with his slow smile]

"'Ere's Mrs. Bradmere, comin' from the Rectory."

[With queer malice]

She don't like cats. But she'm a cat 'erself, I think.

STRANGWAY [With his smile]
Jim!

JIM
She'm always tellin' me I'm lukin' better. I'm not better, zurr.

STRANGWAY
That's her kindness.

JIM
I don't think it is. 'Tis laziness, an' 'avin' 'er own way. She'm very fond of 'er own way.

[A knock on the door cuts off his speech. Following closely on the knock, as though no doors were licensed to be closed against her, a grey-haired lady enters; a capable, broad-faced woman of seventy, whose every tone and movement exhales authority. With a nod and a "good morning" to **STRANGWAY** she turns at face to **JIM BERE**.]

MRS BRADMERE
Ah! Jim; you're looking better.

[**JIM BERE** shakes his head.

MRS BRADMERE
Oh! yes, you are.
Getting on splendidly. And now, I just want to speak to Mr. Strangway.]

[**JIM BERE** touches his forelock, and slowly, leaning on his stick, goes out.]

MRS BRADMERE [Waiting for the door to close]
You know how that came on him? Caught the girl he was engaged to, one night, with another man, the rage broke something here.

[She touches her forehead]

Four years ago.

STRANGWAY
Poor fellow!

MRS BRADMERE [Looking at him sharply]
Is your wife back?

STRANGWAY [Starting]
No.

MRS BRADMERE
By the way, poor Mrs. Cremer—is she any better?

STRANGWAY
No; going fast: Wonderful—so patient.

MRS BRADMERE [With gruff sympathy]
Um! Yes. They know how to die!

[Wide another sharp look at him]

D'you expect your wife soon?

STRANGWAY
I I—hope so.

MRS BRADMERE
So do I. The sooner the better.

STRANGWAY [Shrinking]
I trust the Rector's not suffering so much this morning?

MRS BRADMERE
Thank you! His foot's very bad.

[As she speaks **MRS BURLACOMBE** returns with a large pale-blue book in her bared.]

MRS BURLACOMBE
Good day, M'm!

[Taking the book across to **STRANGWAY**]

Miss Willie, she says she'm very sorry, zurr.

STRANGWAY
She was very welcome, Mrs. Burlacombe. [To **MRS BURLACOMBE**] Forgive me—my sermon.

[He goes into the house. The two **WOMEN** graze after him. Then, at once, as it were, draw into themselves, as if preparing for an encounter, and yet seem to expand as if losing the need for restraint.]

MRS BRADMERE [Abruptly]
He misses his wife very much, I'm afraid.

MRS BURLACOMBE
Ah! Don't he? Poor dear man; he keeps a terrible tight 'and over 'imself, but 'tis suthin' cruel the way he walks about at night. He'm just like a cow when its calf's weaned. 'T'as gone to me 'eart truly to see 'im these months past. T'other day when I went up to du his rume, I yeard a noise like this [she sniffs]; an' ther' 'e was at the wardrobe, snuffin' at 'er things. I did never think a man cud care for a woman so much as that.

MRS BRADMERE
H'm!

MRS BURLACOMBE
'Tis funny rest an' 'e comin' 'ere for quiet after that tearin' great London parish! 'E'm terrible absent-minded tu —don't take no interest in 'is fude. Yesterday, goin' on for one o'clock, 'e says to me, "I expect 'tis nearly breakfast-time, Mrs. Burlacombe!" 'E'd 'ad it twice already!

MRS BRADMERE
Twice! Nonsense!

MRS BURLACOMBE
Zurely! I give 'im a nummit afore 'e gets up; an' 'e 'as 'is brekjus reg'lar at nine. Must feed un up. He'm on 'is feet all day, gain' to zee folk that widden want to zee an angel, they're that busy; an' when 'e comes in 'e'll play 'is flute there. Hem wastin' away for want of 'is wife. That's what 'tis. An' 'im so sweet-spoken, tu, 'tes a pleasure to year 'im—Never says a word!

MRS BRADMERE
Yes, that's the kind of man who gets treated badly. I'm afraid she's not worthy of him, Mrs. Burlacombe.

MRS BURLACOMBE [Plaiting her apron]
'Tesn't for me to zay that. She'm a very pleasant lady.

MRS BRADMERE
Too pleasant. What's this story about her being seen in Durford?

MRS BURLACOMBE
Aw! I du never year no gossip, m'm.

MRS BRADMERE [Drily]
Of course not! But you see the Rector wishes to know.

MRS BURLACOMBE [Flustered]

Well—folk will talk! But, as I says to Burlacombe—"'Tes paltry," I says; and they only married eighteen months, and Mr. Strangway so devoted-like. 'Tes nothing but love, with 'im.

MRS BRADMERE
Come!

MRS BURLACOMBE
There's puzzivantin' folk as'll set an' gossip the feathers off an angel. But I du never listen.

MRS BRADMERE
Now then, Mrs. Burlacombe?

MRS BURLACOMBE
Well, they du say as how Dr. Desart over to Durford and Mrs. Strangway was sweethearts afore she wer' married.

MRS BRADMERE
I knew that. Who was it saw her coming out of Dr. Desart's house yesterday?

MRS BURLACOMBE
In a manner of spakin' 'tes Mrs. Freman that says 'er Gladys seen her.

MRS BRADMERE
That child's got an eye like a hawk.

MRS BURLACOMBE
'Tes wonderful how things du spread. 'Tesn't as if us gossiped. Du seem to grow-like in the naight.

MRS BRADMERE [To herself]
I never lied her. That Riviera excuse, Mrs. Burlacombe—Very convenient things, sick mothers. Mr. Strangway doesn't know?

MRS BURLACOMBE
The Lord forbid! 'Twid send un crazy, I think. For all he'm so moony an' gentlelike, I think he'm a terrible passionate man inside. He've a-got a saint in 'im, for zure; but 'tes only 'alf-baked, in a manner of spakin'.

MRS BRADMERE
I shall go and see Mrs. Freman. There's been too much of this gossip all the winter.

MRS BURLACOMBE
'Tes unfortunate-like 'tes the Fremans. Freman he'm a gipsy sort of a feller; and he've never forgiven Mr. Strangway for spakin' to 'im about the way he trates 'is 'orses.

MRS BRADMERE
Ah! I'm afraid Mr. Strangway's not too discreet when his feelings are touched.

MRS BURLACOMBE

'E've a-got an 'eart so big as the full mune. But 'tes no yuse espectin' tu much o' this world. 'Tes a funny place, after that.

MRS BRADMERE
Yes, Mrs. Burlacombe; and I shall give some of these good people a rare rap over the knuckles for their want of charity. For all they look as if butter wouldn't melt in their mouths, they're an un-Christian lot. [Looking very directly at **MRS BURLACOMBE**] It's lucky we've some hold over the village. I'm not going to have scandal. I shall speak to Sir Herbert, and he and the Rector will take steps.

MRS BURLACOMBE [With covert malice]
Aw! I du hope 'twon't upset the Rector, an' 'is fute so poptious!

MRS BRADMERE [Grimly]
His foot'll be sound enough to come down sharp. By the way, will you send me a duck up to the Rectory?

MRS BURLACOMBE [Glad to get away]
Zurely, m'm; at once. I've some luv'ly fat birds.

[She goes into the house.]

MRS BRADMERE
Old puss-cat!

[She turns to go, and in the doorway encounters a very little, red-cheeked **GIRL** in a peacock-blue cap, and pink frock, who curtsies stolidly.]

MRS BRADMERE
Well, Tibby Jarland, what do you want here? Always
sucking something, aren't you?

[Getting no reply from **TIBBY JARLAND**, she passes out. **TIBBT** comes in, looks round, takes a large sweet out of her mouth, contemplates it, and puts it back again. Then, in a perfunctory and very stolid fashion, she looks about the floor, as if she had been told to find something. While she is finding nothing and sucking her sweet, her sister **MERCY** comes in furtively, still frowning and vindictive.]

MERCY
What! Haven't you found it, Tibby? Get along with 'ee, then!

[She accelerates the stolid **TIBBY'S** departure with a smack, searches under the seat, finds and picks up the deserted sixpence. Then very quickly she goes to the door: But it is opened before she reaches it, and, finding herself caught, she slips behind the chintz window-curtain. A **WOMAN** has entered, who is clearly the original of the large photograph. She is not strictly pretty, but there is charm in her pale, resolute face, with its mocking lips, flexible brows, and greenish eyes, whose lids, square above them, have short, dark lashes. She is dressed in blue, and her fair hair is coiled up under a cap and motor-veil. She comes in swiftly, and closes the door behind her; becomes irresolute; then, suddenly deciding, moves towards the door into the house. **MERCY** slips from behind her curtain to make off, but at that moment the door into the house is opened, and she has at once to slip back again into covert. It is **IVY** who has appeared.]

IVY [Amazed]
Oh! Mrs. Strangway!

[Evidently disconcerted by this appearance, **BEATRICE STRANGWAY** pulls herself together and confronts the child with a smile.]

BEATRICE
Well, Ivy—you've grown! You didn't expect me, did you?

IVY
No, Mrs. Strangway; but I hoped yu'd be comin' soon.

BEATRICE
Ah! Yes. Is Mr. Strangway in?

IVY [Hypnotized by those faintly smiling lips]
Yes—oh, yes! He's writin' his sermon in the little room. He will be glad!

BEATRICE [Going a little closer, and never taking her eyes off the child]
Yes. Now, Ivy; will you do something for me?

IVY [Fluttering]
Oh, yes, Mrs. Strangway.

BEATRICE
Quite sure?

IVY
Oh, yes!

BEATRICE
Are you old enough to keep a secret?

IVY [Nodding]
I'm fourteen now.

BEATRICE
Well, then—, I don't want anybody but Mr. Strangway to know I've been here; nobody, not even your mother. D'you understand?

IVY [Troubled]
No. Only, I can keep a secret.

BEATRICE
Mind, if anybody hears, it will hurt Mr. Strangway.

IVY

Oh! I wouldn't—hurt—him. Must yu go away again? [Trembling towards her] I wish yu wer goin' to stay. And perhaps some one has seen yu—They—

BEATRICE [Hastily]

No, no one. I came motoring; like this.

[She moves her veil to show how it can conceal her face]

And I came straight down the little lane, and through the barn, across the yard.

IVY [Timidly]

People du see a lot.

BEATRICE [Still with that hovering smile]

I know, but—Now go and tell him quickly and quietly.

IVY [Stopping at the door]

Mother's pluckin' a duck. Only, please, Mrs. Strangway, if she comes in even after yu've gone, she'll know, because—because yu always have that particular nice scent.

BEATRICE

Thank you, my child. I'll see to that.

[**IVY** looks at her as if she would speak again, then turns suddenly, and goes out. **BEATRICE'S** face darkens; she shivers. Taking out a little cigarette case, she lights a cigarette, and watches the puff's of smoke wreathe shout her and die away. The frightened **MERCY** peers out, spying for a chance, to escape. Then from the house **STRANGWAY** comes in. All his dreaminess is gone.]

STRANGWAY

Thank God!

[He stops at the look on her face]

I don't understand, though. I thought you were still out there.

BEATRICE [Letting her cigarette fall, and putting her foot on it]

No.

STRANGWAY

You're staying? Oh! Beatrice; come! We'll get away from here at once—as far, as far—anywhere you like. Oh! my darling —only come! If you knew—

BEATRICE

It's no good, Michael; I've tried and tried.

STRANGWAY

Not! Then, why—? Beatrice! You said, when you were right away—I've waited—

BEATRICE
I know. It's cruel—it's horrible. But I told you not to hope, Michael. I've done my best. All these months at Mentone, I've been wondering why I ever let you marry me—when that feeling wasn't dead!

STRANGWAY
You can't have come back just to leave me again?

BEATRICE
When you let me go out there with mother I thought—I did think I would be able; and I had begun—and then—spring came!

STRANGWAY
Spring came here too! Never so—aching! Beatrice, can't you?

BEATRICE
I've something to say.

STRANGWAY
No! No! No!

BEATRICE
You see—I've—fallen.

STRANGWAY
Ah! [In a thrice sharpened by pain] Why, in the name of mercy, come here to tell me that? Was he out there, then?

BEATRICE
I came straight back to him.

STRANGWAY
To Durford?

BEATRICE
To the Crossway Hotel, miles out—in my own name. They don't know me there. I told you not to hope, Michael. I've done my best; I swear it.

STRANGWAY
My God!

BEATRICE
It was your God that brought us to live near him!

STRANGWAY
Why have you come to me like this?

BEATRICE
To know what you're going to do. Are you going to divorce me? We're in your power. Don't divorce me—Doctor and patient—you must know—it ruins him. He'll lose everything. He'd be disqualified, and he hasn't a penny without his work.

STRANGWAY
Why should I spare him?

BEATRICE
Michael; I came to beg. It's hard.

STRANGWAY
No; don't beg! I can't stand it.

[She shakes her head.]

BEATRICE [Recovering her pride]
What are you going to do, then? Keep us apart by the threat of a divorce? Starve us and prison us? Cage me up here with you? I'm not brute enough to ruin him.

STRANGWAY
Heaven!

BEATRICE
I never really stopped loving him. I never—loved you, Michael.

STRANGWAY [Stunned]

Is that true?

[**BEATRICE** bends her head]

Never loved me? Not—that night—on the river—not—?

BEATRICE
[Under her breath] No.

STRANGWAY
Were you lying to me, then? Kissing me, and—hating me?

BEATRICE
One doesn't hate men like you; but it wasn't love.

STRANGWAY
Why did you tell me it was?

BEATRICE
Yes. That was the worst thing I've ever done.

STRANGWAY
Do you think I would have married you? I would have burned first! I never dreamed you didn't. I swear it!

BEATRICE [Very low]
Forget it!

STRANGWAY
Did he try to get you away from me?

[**BEATRICE** gives him a swift look]

Tell me the truth!

BEATRICE
No. It was—I—alone. But—he loves me.

STRANGWAY
One does not easily know love, it seems.

[But her smile, faint, mysterious, pitying, is enough, and he turns away from her.]

BEATRICE
It was cruel to come, I know. For me, too. But I couldn't write. I had to know.

STRANGWAY
Never loved me? Never loved me? That night at Tregaron? [At the look on her face] You might have told me before you went away! Why keep me all these—

BEATRICE
I meant to forget him again. I did mean to. I thought I could get back to what I was, when I married you; but, you see, what a girl can do, a woman that's been married—can't.

STRANGWAY
Then it was I—my kisses that—!

[He laughs]

How did you stand them?

[His eyes dart at her face]

Imagination helped you, perhaps!

BEATRICE
Michael, don't, don't! And—oh! don't make a public thing of it! You needn't be afraid I shall have too good a time!

[He stays quite still and silent, and that which is writhing in him makes his face so strange that **BEATRICE** stands aghast. At last she goes stumbling on in speech]

If ever you want to marry some one else—then, of course—that's only fair, ruin or not. But till then—till then—He's leaving Durford, going to Brighton. No one need know. And you—this isn't the only parish in the world.

STRANGWAY [Quietly]
You ask me to help you live in secret with another man?

BEATRICE
I ask for mercy.

STRANGWAY [As to himself]
What am I to do?

BEATRICE
What you feel in the bottom of your heart.

STRANGWAY
You ask me to help you live in sin?

BEATRICE
To let me go out of your life. You've only to do—nothing.

[He goes, slowly, close to her.]

STRANGWAY
I want you. Come back to me! Beatrice, come back!

BEATRICE
It would be torture, now.

STRANGWAY [Writhing]
Oh!

BEATRICE
Whatever's in your heart—do!

STRANGWAY
You'd come back to me sooner than ruin him? Would you?

BEATRICE
I can't bring him harm.

STRANGWAY [Turning away]
God!—if there be one help me!

[He stands leaning his forehead against the window. Suddenly his glance falls on the little bird cage, still lying on the window-seat]

Never cage any wild thing!

[He gives a laugh that is half a sob; then, turning to the door, says in a low voice]

Go! Go please, quickly! Do what you will. I won't hurt you—can't—But—go!

[He opens the door.]

BEATRICE [Greatly moved]
Thank you!

[She passes him with her head down, and goes out quickly. **STRANGWAY** stands unconsciously tearing at the little bird-cage. And while he tears at it he utters a moaning sound. The terrified **MERCY**, peering from behind the curtain, and watching her chance, slips to the still open door; but in her haste and fright she knocks against it, and **STRANGWAY** sees her. Before he can stop her she has fled out on to the green and away.]

[While he stands there, paralysed, the door from the house is opened, and **MRS BURLACOMBE** approaches him in a queer, hushed way.]

MRS BURLACOMBE [Her eyes mechanically fixed on the twisted bird-cage in his hands]
'Tis poor Sue Cremer, zurr, I didn't 'ardly think she'd last thru the mornin'. An' zure enough she'm passed away!

[Seeing that he has not taken in her words]

Mr. Strangway— yu'm feelin' giddy?

STRANGWAY
No, no! What was it? You said—

MRS BURLACOMBE
'Tes Jack Cremer. His wife's gone. 'E'm in a terrible way. 'Tes only yu, 'e ses, can du 'im any gude. He'm in the kitchen.

STRANGWAY
Cremer? Yes! Of course. Let him—

MRS BURLACOMBE [Still staring at the twisted cage]
Yu ain't wantin' that—'tes all twizzled.

[She takes it from him]

Sure yu'm not feelin' yer 'ead?

STRANGWAY [With a resolute effort]

No!

MRS BURLACOMBE [Doubtfully]

I'll send 'im in, then.

[She goes. When she is gone, **STRANGWAY** passes his handkerchief across his forehead, and his lips move fast. He is standing motionless when **CREMER**, a big man in labourer's clothes, with a thick, broad face, and tragic, faithful eyes, comes in, and stands a little in from the closed door, quite dumb.]

STRANGWAY [After a moment's silence—going up to him and laying a hand on his shoulder]

Jack! Don't give way. If we give way—we're done.

CREMER

Yes, zurr.

[A quiver passes over his face.]

STRANGWAY

She didn't. Your wife was a brave woman. A dear woman.

CREMER

I never thought to luse 'er. She never told me 'ow bad she was, afore she tuk to 'er bed. 'Tis a dreadful thing to luse a wife, zurr.

STRANGWAY [Tightening his lips, that tremble]

Yes. But don't give way! Bear up, Jack!

CREMER

Seems funny 'er goin' blue-bell time, an' the sun shinin' so warm. I picked up an 'orse-shu yesterday. I can't never 'ave 'er back, zurr.

[His face quivers again.]

STRANGWAY

Some day you'll join her. Think! Some lose their wives for ever.

CREMER

I don't believe as there's a future life, zurr. I think we goo to sleep like the beasts.

STRANGWAY

We're told otherwise. But come here!

[Drawing him to the window]

Look! Listen! To sleep in that! Even if we do, it won't be so bad, Jack, will it?

CREMER
She wer' a gude wife to me—no man didn't 'ave no better wife.

STRANGWAY [Putting his hand out]
Take hold—hard—harder! I want yours as much as you want mine. Pray for me, Jack, and I'll pray for you. And we won't give way, will we?

CREMER [To whom the strangeness of these words has given some relief]
No, zurr; thank 'ee, zurr. 'Tes no gude, I expect. Only, I'll miss 'er. Thank 'ee, zurr; kindly.

[He lifts his hand to his head, turns, and uncertainly goes out to the kitchen. And **STRANGWAY** stays where he is, not knowing what to do. They blindly he takes up his flute, and hatless, hurries out into the air.]

ACT II

SCENE I

About seven o'clock in the taproom of the village inn. The bar, with the appurtenances thereof, stretches across one end, and opposite is the porch door on to the green. The wall between is nearly all window, with leaded panes, one wide-open casement whereof lets in the last of the sunlight. A narrow bench runs under this broad window. And this is all the furniture, save three spittoons:

GODLEIGH, the innkeeper, a smallish man with thick ruffled hair, a loquacious nose, and apple-red cheeks above a reddish-brown moustache; is reading the paper. To him enters **TIBBY JARLAND** with a shilling in her mouth.

GODLEIGH
Well, Tibby Jarland, what've yu come for, then? Glass o' beer?

[**TIBBY** takes the shilling from her mouth and smiles stolidly.]

GODLEIGH [Twinkling]
I shid zay glass o' 'arf an' 'arf's about yure form.

[**TIBBY** smiles more broadly]

Yu'm a praaper masterpiece. Well! 'Ave sister Mercy borrowed yure tongue?

[**TIBBY** shakes her head]

Aw, she 'aven't. Well, maid?

TIBBY
Father wants six clay pipes, please.

GODLEIGH
'E du, du 'ee? Yu tell yure father 'e can't 'ave more'n one, not this avenin'. And 'ere 'tis. Hand up yure shillin'.

[**TIBBY** reaches up her hand, parts with the shilling, and receives a long clay pipe and eleven pennies. In order to secure the coins in her pinafore she places the clay pipe in her mouth. While she is still thus engaged, **MRS BRADMERE** enters the porch and comes in. **TIBBY** curtsies stolidly.]

MRS BRADMERE
Gracious, child! What are you doing here? And what have you got in your mouth? Who is it? Tibby Jarland?

[**TIBBY** curtsies again]

Take that thing out. And tell your father from me that if I ever see you at the inn again I shall tread on his toes hard. Godleigh, you know the law about children?

GODLEIGH [Cocking his eye, and not at all abashed]
Surely, m'm. But she will come. Go away, my dear.

[**TIBBY**, never taking her eyes off **MRS BRADMERE**, or the pipe from her mouth, has backed stolidly to the door, and vanished.]

MRS BRADMERE [Eyeing **GODLEIGH**]
Now, Godleigh, I've come to talk to you. Half the scandal that goes about the village begins here.

[She holds up her finger to check expostulation]

No, no—its no good. You know the value of scandal to your business far too well.

GODLEIGH
Wi' all respect, m'm, I knows the vally of it to yourn, tu.

MRS BRADMERE
What do you mean by that?

GODLEIGH
If there weren't no Rector's lady there widden' be no notice taken o' scandal; an' if there weren't no notice taken, twidden be scandal, to my thinkin'.

MRS BRADMERE [Winking out a grim little smile]
Very well! You've given me your views. Now for mine. There's a piece of scandal going about that's got to be stopped, Godleigh. You turn the tap of it off here, or we'll turn your tap off. You know me. See?

GODLEIGH

I shouldn' never presume, m'm, to know a lady.

MRS BRADMERE
The Rector's quite determined, so is Sir Herbert. Ordinary scandal's bad enough, but this touches the Church. While Mr. Strangway remains curate here, there must be no talk about him and his affairs.

GODLEIGH [Cocking his eye]
I was just thinkin' how to du it, m'm. 'Twid be a brave notion to putt the men in chokey, and slit the women's tongues-like, same as they du in outlandish places, as I'm told.

MRS BRADMERE
Don't talk nonsense, Godleigh; and mind what I say, because I mean it.

GODLEIGH
Make yure mind aisy, m'm there'll be no scandal-monkeyin' here wi' my permission.

[**MRS BRADMERE** gives him a keen stare, but seeing him perfectly grave, nods her head with approval.]

MRS BRADMERE
Good! You know what's being said, of course?

GODLEIGH [With respectful gravity]
Yu'll pardon me, m'm, but ef an' in case yu was goin' to tell me, there's a rule in this 'ouse: "No scandal 'ere!"

MRS BRADMERE [Twinkling grimly]
You're too smart by half, my man.

GODLEIGH
Aw fegs, no, m'm—child in yure 'ands.

MRS BRADMERE
I wouldn't trust you a yard. Once more, Godleigh! This is a Christian village, and we mean it to remain so. You look out for yourself.

[The door opens to admit the farmers **TRUSTAFORD** and **BURLACOMBE**. They doff their hats to **MRS** BRADMERE, who, after one more sharp look at **GODLEIGH**, moves towards the door.]

MRS BRADMERE
Evening, Mr. Trustaford. [To **BURLACOMBE**] Burlacombe, tell your wife that duck she sent up was in hard training.

[With one of her grim winks, and a nod, she goes.]

TRUSTAFORD [Replacing a hat which is black, hard, and not very new, on his long head, above a long face, clean-shaved but for little whiskers]
What's the old grey mare want, then? [With a horse-laugh] 'Er's lukin' awful wise!

GODLEIGH [Enigmatically]
Ah!

TRUSTAFORD [Sitting on the bench dose to the bar]
Drop o' whisky, an' potash.

BURLACOMBE [A taciturn, alien, yellowish man, in a worn soft hat]
What's wise, Godleigh? Drop o' cider.

GODLEIGH
Nuse? There's never no nuse in this 'ouse. Aw, no! Not wi' my permission. [In imitation] This is a Christian village.

TRUSTAFORD
Thought the old grey mare seemed mighty busy. [To **BURLACOMBE**] 'Tes rather quare about the curate's wife a-cumin' motorin' this mornin'. Passed me wi' her face all smothered up in a veil, goggles an' all. Haw, haw!

BURLACOMBE
Aye!

TRUSTAFORD
Off again she was in 'alf an hour. 'Er didn't give poor old curate much of a chance, after six months.

GODLEIGH
Havin' an engagement elsewhere—No scandal, please, gentlemen.

BURLACOMBE [Acidly]
Never asked to see my missis. Passed me in the yard like a stone.

TRUSTAFORD
'Tes a little bit rumoursome lately about 'er doctor.

GODLEIGH
Ah! he's the favourite. But 'tes a dead secret; Mr. Trustaford. Don't yu never repate it—there's not a cat don't know it already!

[**BURLACOMBE** frowns, and **TRUSTAFORD** utters his laugh. The door is opened and **FREMAN**, a dark gipsyish man in the dress of a farmer, comes in.

GODLEIGH
Don't yu never tell Will Freman what 'e told me!

FREMAN
Avenin'!

TRUSTAFORD
Avenin', Will; what's yure glass o' trouble?

FREMAN

Drop o' eider, clove, an' dash o' gin. There's blood in the sky to-night.

BURLACOMBE

Ah! We'll 'ave fine weather now, with the full o' the mune.

FREMAN

Dust o' wind an' a drop or tu, virst, I reckon. 'Earl t' nuse about curate an' 'is wife?

GODLEIGH

No, indeed; an' don't yu tell us. We'm Christians 'ere in this village.

FREMAN

'Tain't no very Christian nuse, neither. He's sent 'er off to th' doctor. "Go an' live with un," 'e says; "my blessin' on ye." If 'er'd a-been mine, I'd 'a tuk the whip to 'er. Tam Jarland's maid, she yeard it all. Christian, indeed! That's brave Christianity! "Goo an' live with un!" 'e told 'er.

BURLACOMBE

No, no; that's, not sense—a man to say that. I'll not 'ear that against a man that bides in my 'ouse.

FREMAN

'Tes sure, I tell 'ee. The maid was hid-up, scared-like, behind the curtain. At it they went, and parson 'e says: "Go," 'e says, "I won't kape 'ee from 'im," 'e says, "an' I won't divorce 'ee, as yu don't wish it!" They was 'is words, same as Jarland's maid told my maid, an' my maid told my missis. If that's parson's talk, 'tes funny work goin' to church.

TRUSTAFORD [Brooding]

'Tes wonderful quare, zurely.

FREMAN

Tam Jarland's fair mad wi' curate for makin' free wi' his maid's skylark. Parson or no parson, 'e've no call to meddle wi' other people's praperty. He cam' pokin' 'is nose into my affairs. I told un I knew a sight more 'bout 'orses than 'e ever would!

TRUSTAFORD

He'm a bit crazy 'bout bastes an' birds.

[They have been so absorbed that they bane not noticed the entrance of **CLYST**, a youth with tousled hair, and a bright, quick, Celtic eye, who stands listening, with a bit of paper in his hand.]

CLYST

Ah! he'm that zurely, Mr. Trustaford.

[He chuckles.]

GODLEIGH

Now, Tim Clyst, if an' in case yu've a-got some scandal on yer tongue, don't yu never unship it here. Yu go up to Rectory where 'twill be more relished-like.

CLYST [Waving the paper]
Will y' give me a drink for this, Mr. Godleigh? 'Tes rale funny. Aw! 'tes somethin' swats. Butiful readin'. Poetry. Rale spice. Yu've a luv'ly voice for readin', Mr. Godleigh.

GODLEIGH [All ears and twinkle]
Aw, what is it then?

CLYST
Ah! Yu want t'know tu much.

[Putting the paper in his pocket.]

[While he is speaking, **JIM BERE** has entered quietly, with his feeble step and smile, and sits down.]

CLYST [Kindly]
Hello, Jim! Cat come 'ome?

JIM BERE
No.

[All nod, and speak to him kindly. And **JIM BERE** smiles at them, and his eyes ask of them the question, to which there is no answer. And after that he sits motionless and silent, and they talk as if he were not there.]

GODLEIGH
What's all this, now—no scandal in my 'ouse!

CLYST
'Tes awful peculiar—like a drame. Mr. Burlacombe 'e don't like to hear tell about drames. A guess a won't tell 'ee, arter that.

FREMAN
Out wi' it, Tim.

CLYST
'Tes powerful thirsty to-day, Mr. Godleigh.

GODLEIGH [Drawing him some cider]
Yu're all wild cat's talk, Tim; yu've a-got no tale at all.

CLYST [Moving for the cider]
Aw, indade!

GODLEIGH
No tale, no cider!

CLYST
Did ye ever year tell of Orphus?

TRUSTAFORD
What? The old vet. up to Drayleigh?

CLYST
Fegs, no; Orphus that lived in th' old time, an' drawed the bastes after un wi' his music, same as curate was tellin' the maids.

FREMAN
I've 'eard as a gipsy over to Vellacott could du that wi' 'is viddle.

CLYST
'Twas no gipsy I see'd this arternune; 'twee Orphus, down to Mr. Burlacombe's long medder; settin' there all dark on a stone among the dimsy-white flowers an' the cowflops, wi' a bird upon 'is 'ead, playin' his whistle to the ponies.

FREMAN [Excitedly]
Yu did never zee a man wi' a bird on 'is 'ead.

CLYST
Didn' I?

FREMAN
What sort o' bird, then? Yu tell me that.

TRUSTAFORD
Praaper old barndoor cock. Haw, haw!

GODLEIGH [Soothingly]
'Tes a vairy-tale; us mustn't be tu partic'lar.

BURLACOMBE
In my long medder? Where were yu, then, Tim Clyst?

CLYST
Passin' down the lane on my bike. Wonderful sorrowful-fine music 'e played. The ponies they did come round 'e—yu cud zee the tears rennin' down their chakes; 'twas powerful sad. 'E 'adn't no 'at on.

FREMAN [Jeering]
No; 'e 'ad a bird on 'is 'ead.

CLYST [With a silencing grin]
He went on playin' an' playin'. The ponies they never muved. An' all the dimsy-white flowers they waved and waved, an' the wind it went over 'em. Gav' me a funny feelin'.

GODLEIGH
Clyst, yu take the cherry bun!

CLYST
Where's that cider, Mr. Godleigh?

GODLEIGH [Bending over the cider]
Yu've a— 'ad tu much already, Tim.

[The door is opened, and **TAM JARLAND** appears. He walks rather unsteadily; a man with a hearty jowl, and sullen, strange; epileptic-looking eyes.]

CLYST [Pointing to **JARLAND**]
'Tis Tam Jarland there 'as the cargo aboard.

JARLAND
Avenin', all! [To **GODLEIGH**] Pinto' beer. [To **JIM BERE**] Avenin', Jim.

[**JIM BERE** looks at him and smiles.]

GODLEIGH [Serving him after a moment's hesitation]
'Ere y'are, Tam. [To **CLYST**, who has taken out his paper again] Where'd yu get thiccy paper?

CLYST [Putting down his cider-mug empty]
Yure tongue du watter, don't it, Mr. Godleigh? [Holding out his mug] No zider, no poetry. 'Tis amazin' sorrowful; Shakespeare over again. "The boy stude on the burnin' deck."

FREMAN
Yu and yer yap!

CLYST
Ah! Yu wait a bit. When I come back down t'lane again, Orphus 'e was vanished away; there was naught in the field but the ponies, an' a praaper old magpie, a-top o' the hedge. I zee somethin' white in the beak o' the fowl, so I giv' a "Whisht," an' 'e drops it smart, an' off 'e go. I gets over bank an' picks un up, and here't be.

[He holds out his mug.]

BURLACOMBE [Tartly]
Here, give 'im 'is cider. Rade it yureself, ye young teasewings.

[**CLYST**, having secured his cider, drinks it up. Holding up the paper to the light, he makes as if to begin, then slides his eye round, tantalizing.]

CLYST
'Tes a pity I bain't dressed in a white gown, an' flowers in
me 'air.

FREMAN
Read it, or we'll 'aye yu out o' this.

CLYST
Aw, don't 'ee shake my nerve, now!

[He begins reading with mock heroism, in his soft, high, burring voice. Thus, in his rustic accent, go the lines]

God lighted the zun in 'eaven far.
Lighted the virefly an' the star.
My 'eart 'E lighted not!

God lighted the vields fur lambs to play,
Lighted the bright strames, 'an the may.
My 'eart 'E lighted not!

God lighted the mune, the Arab's way,
He lights to-morrer, an' to-day.
My 'eart 'E 'ath vorgot!

[When he has finished, there is silence. Then **TRUSTAFORD**, scratching his head, speaks:]

TAUSTAFORD
'Tes amazin' funny stuff.

FREMAN [Looking over **CLYST'S** shoulder]
Be danged! 'Tes the curate's 'andwritin'. 'Twas curate wi' the ponies, after that.

CLYST
Fancy, now! Aw, Will Freman, an't yu bright!

FREMAN
But 'e 'adn't no bird on 'is 'ead.

CLYST
Ya-as, 'e 'ad.

JARLAND [In a dull, threatening voice]
'E 'ad my maid's bird, this arternune. 'Ead or no, and parson or no, I'll gie 'im one for that.

FREMAN
Ah! And 'e meddled wi' my 'orses.

TRUSTAFORD
I'm thinkin' 'twas an old cuckoo bird 'e 'ad on 'is 'ead. Haw, haw!

GODLEIGH

"His 'eart She 'ath Vorgot!"

FREMAN
'E's a fine one to be tachin' our maids convirmation.

GODLEIGH
Would ye 'ave it the old Rector then? Wi' 'is gouty shoe? Rackon the maids wid rather 'twas curate; eh, Mr. Burlacombe?

BURLACOMBE [Abruptly]
Curate's a gude man.

JARLAND [With the comatose ferocity of drink]
I'll be even wi' un.

FREMAN [Excitedly]
Tell 'ee one thing—'tes not a proper man o' God to 'ave about, wi' 'is luse goin's on. Out vrom 'ere he oughter go.

BURLACOMBE
You med go further an' fare worse.

FREMAN
What's 'e duin', then, lettin' 'is wife runoff?

TRUSTAFORD [Scratching his head]
If an' in case 'e can't kape 'er, 'tes a funny way o' duin' things not to divorce 'er, after that. If a parson's not to du the Christian thing, whu is, then?

BURLACOMBE
'Tes a bit immoral-like to pass over a thing like that. Tes funny if women's gain's on's to be encouraged.

FREMAN
Act of a coward, I zay.

BURLACOMBE
The curate ain't no coward.

FREMAN
He bides in yure house; 'tes natural for yu to stand up for un; I'll wager Mrs. Burlacombe don't, though. My missis was fair shocked. "Will," she says, "if yu ever make vur to let me go like that, I widden never stay wi' yu," she says.

TRUSTAFORD
'Tes settin' a bad example, for zure.

BURLACOMBE
'Tes all very airy talkin'; what shude 'e du, then?

FREMAN [Excitedly]

Go over to Durford and say to that doctor: "Yu come about my missis, an' zee what I'll du to 'ee." An' take 'er 'ome an' zee she don't misbe'ave again.

CLYST

'E can't take 'er ef 'er don' want t' come—I've 'eard lawyer, that lodged wi' us, say that.

FREMAN

All right then, 'e ought to 'ave the law of 'er and 'er doctor; an' zee 'er goin's on don't prosper; 'e'd get damages, tu. But this way 'tes a nice example he'm settin' folks. Parson indade! My missis an' the maids they won't goo near the church to-night, an' I wager no one else won't, neither.

JARLAND [Lurching with his pewter up to **GODLEIGH**]

The beggar! I'll be even wi' un.

GODLEIGH [Looking at him in doubt]

'Tes the last, then, Tam.

[Having received his beer, **JARLAND** stands, leaning against the bar, drinking.]

BURLACOMBE [Suddenly]

I don' goo with what curate's duin—'tes tiff soft 'earted; he'm a muney kind o' man altogether, wi' 'is flute an' 'is poetry; but he've a-lodged in my 'ouse this year an' mare, and always 'ad an 'elpin' 'and for every one. I've got a likin' for him an' there's an end of it.

JARLAND

The coward!

TRUSTAFORD

I don' trouble nothin' about that, Tam Jarland. [Turning to **BURLACOMBE**] What gits me is 'e don't seem to 'ave no zense o' what's his own praperty.

JARLAND

Take other folk's property fast enough!

[He saws the air with his empty. The others have all turned to him, drawn by the fascination that a man in liquor has for his fellow-men. The bell for church has begun to rang, the sun is down, and it is getting dusk.]

He wants one on his crop, an' one in 'is belly; 'e wants a man to take an' gie un a gude hidin zame as he oughter give 'is fly-be-night of a wife.

[**STRANGWAY** in his dark clothes has entered, and stands by the door, his lips compressed to a colourless line, his thin, darkish face grey-white]

Zame as a man wid ha' gi'en the doctor, for takin' what isn't his'n.

[All but **JARLAND** have seen **STRANGWAY**. He steps forward, **JARLAND** sees him now; his jaw drops a little, and he is silent.

STRANGWAY
I came for a little brandy, Mr. Godleigh—feeling rather faint. Afraid I mightn't get through the service.

GODLEIGH [With professional composure]
Marteil's Three Star, zurr, or 'Ennessy's?

STRANGWAY [Looking at **JARLAND**]
Thank you; I believe I can do without, now.

[He turns to go.]

[In the deadly silence, **GODLEIGH** touches the arm of **JARLAND**, who, leaning against the bar with the pewter in his hand, is staring with his strange lowering eyes straight at **STRANGWAY**.]

JARLAND [Galvanized by the touch into drunken rage]
Lave me be—I'll talk to un-parson or no. I'll tache un to meddle wi' my maid's bird. I'll tache un to kape 'is thievin' 'ands to 'imself.

[**STRANGWAY** turns again.]

CLYST
Be quiet, Tam.

JARLAND [Never loosing **STRANGWAY** with his eyes—like a bull-dog who sees red]
That's for one chake; zee un turn t'other, the white-livered buty! Whu lets another man 'ave 'is wife, an' never the sperit to go vor un!

BURLACOMBE
Shame, Jarland; quiet, man!

[They are all looking at **STRANGWAY**, who, under **JARLAND'S** drunken insults is standing rigid, with his eyes closed, and his hands hard clenched. The church bell has stopped slow ringing, and begun its five minutes' hurrying note.]

TRUSTAFORD [Rising, and trying to hook his arm into **JARLAND'S**]
Come away, Tam; yu've a-'ad to much, man.

JARLAND [Shaking him off]
Zee, 'e darsen't touch me; I might 'it un in the vase an' 'e darsen't; 'e's afraid—like 'e was o' the doctor.

[He raises the pewter as though to fling it, but it is seized by **GODLEIGH** from behind, and falls clattering to the floor. **STRANGWAY** has not moved.]

JARLAND [Shaking his fist almost in his face]
Luke at un, Luke at un! A man wi' a slut for a wife—

[As he utters the word "wife" **STRANGWAY** seizes the outstretched fist, and with a jujitsu movement, draws him into his clutch, helpless. And as they sway and struggle in the open window, with the false strength of fury he forces **JARLAND** through. There is a crash of broken glass from outside. At the sound **STRANGWAY** comes to himself. A look of agony passes over his face. His eyes light on **JIM BERE**, who has suddenly risen, and stands feebly clapping his hands. **STRANGWAY** rushes out.]

[Excitedly gathering at the window, they all speak at once.]

CLYST
Tam's hatchin' of yure cucumbers, Mr. Godleigh.

TRUSTAFORD
'E did crash; haw, haw!

FREMAN
'Twas a brave throw, zurely. Whu wid a' thought it?

CLYST
Tam's crawlin' out.

[Leaning through window]

Hello, Tam—'ow's t' base, old man?

FREMAN [Excitedly]
They'm all comin' up from churchyard to zee.

TRUSTAFORD
Tam du luke wonderful aztonished; haw, haw! Poor old Tam!

CLYST
Can yu zee curate? Reckon 'e'm gone into church. Aw, yes; gettin' a bit dimsy-service time.

[A moment's hush.]

TRUSTAFORD
Well, I'm jiggered. In 'alf an hour he'm got to prache.

GODLEIGH
'Tes a Christian village, boys.

[Feebly, quietly, **JIM BERE** laughs. There is silence; but the bell is heard still ranging.]

SCENE II

The same-in daylight dying fast. A lamp is burning on the bar. A chair has been placed in the centre of the room, facing the bench under the window, on which are seated from right to left, **GODLEIGH, SOL POTTER** the village shopman, **TRUSTAFORD, BURLACOMBE, FREMAN, JIM BERE**, and **MORSE** the blacksmith. **CLYST** is squatting on a stool by the bar, and at the other end **JARLAND**, sobered and lowering, leans against the lintel of the porch leading to the door, round which are gathered five or six sturdy **FELLOWS**, dumb as fishes. No one sits in the chair. In the unnatural silence that reigns, the distant sound of the wheezy church organ and voices singing can be heard.

TAUSTAFORD [After a prolonged clearing of his throat]
What I mean to zay is that 'tes no yuse, not a bit o' yuse in the world, not duin' of things properly. If an' in case we'm to carry a resolution disapprovin' o' curate, it must all be done so as no one can't, zay nothin'.

SOL POTTER
That's what I zay, Mr. Trustaford; ef so be as 'tis to be a village meetin', then it must be all done proper.

FREMAN
That's right, Sot Potter. I purpose Mr. Sot Potter into the chair. Whu seconds that?

[A silence. **VOICES** from among the dumb-as-fishes: "I du."]

CLYST [Excitedly]
Yu can't putt that to the meetin'. Only a chairman can putt it to the meetin'. I purpose that Mr. Burlacombe—bein as how he's chairman o' the Parish Council—take the chair.

FREMAN
Ef so be as I can't putt it, yu can't putt that neither.

TRUSTAFORD
'Tes not a bit o' yuse; us can't 'ave no meetin' without a chairman.

GODLEIGH
Us can't 'ave no chairman without a meetin' to elect un, that's zure.

[A silence.]

MORSE [Heavily]
To my way o' thinkin', Mr. Godleigh speaks zense; us must 'ave a meetin' before us can 'ave a chairman.

CLYST
Then what we got to du's to elect a meetin'.

BURLACOMBE [Sourly]
Yu'll not find no procedure far that.

[**VOICES** from among the dumb-as fishes: "Mr. Burlacombe 'e oughter know."]

SOL POTTER [Scratching his head—with heavy solemnity]

'Tes my belief there's no other way to du, but to elect a chairman to call a meetin'; an' then for that meetin' to elect a chairman.

CLYST
I purpose Mr. Burlacombe as chairman to call a meetin'.

FREMAN
I purpose Sol Potter.

GODLEIGH
Can't 'ave tu propositions together before a meetin'; that's apple-pie zure vur zurtain.

[**VOICE** from among the dumb-as fishes: "There ain't no meetin' yet, Sol Potter zays."]

TRUSTAFORD
Us must get the rights of it zettled some'ow. 'Tes like the darned old chicken an' the egg—meetin' or chairman—which come virst?

SOL POTTER [Conciliating]
To my thinkin' there shid be another way o' duin' it, to get round it like with a circumbendibus. 'T'all comes from takin' different vuse, in a manner o' spakin'.

FREMAN
Vu goo an' zet in that chair.

SOL POTTER [With a glance at **BURLACOMBE** modestly]
I shid'n never like fur to du that, with Mr. Burlacombe zettin' there.

BURLACOMBE [Rising]
'Tes all darned fulishness.

[Amidst an uneasy shufflement of feet he moves to the door, and goes out into the darkness.]

CLYST
[Seeing his candidate thus depart]
Rackon curate's pretty well thru by now, I'm goin' to zee.

[As he passes **JARLAND**]

'Ow's to base, old man?

[He goes out. One of the dumb-as-fishes moves from the door and fills the apace left on the bench by **BURLACOMBE'S** departure.]

JARLAND
Darn all this puzzivantin'! [To **SOL POTTER**] Got an' zet in that chair.

SOL POTTER [Rising and going to the chair; there he stands, changing from one to the other of his short broad feet and sweating from modesty and worth]
'Tes my duty now, gentlemen, to call a meetin' of the parishioners of this parish. I beg therefore to declare that this is a meetin' in accordance with my duty as chairman of this meetin' which elected me chairman to call this meetin'. And I purceed to vacate the chair so that this meetin' may now purceed to elect a chairman.

[He gets up from the chair, and wiping the sweat from his brow, goes back to his seat.]

FREMAN
Mr. Chairman, I rise on a point of order.

GODLEIGH
There ain't no chairman.

FREMAN
I don't give a darn for that. I rise on a point of order.

GODLEIGH
'Tes a chairman that decides points of order. 'Tes certain yu can't rise on no points whatever till there's a chairman.

TRUSTAFORD
'Tes no yuse yure risin', not the least bit in the world, till there's some one to set yu down again. Haw, haw!

[**VOICE** from the dumb-as-fishes: "Mr. Trustaford 'e's right."]

FREMAN
What I zay is the chairman ought never to 'ave vacated the chair till I'd risen on my point of order. I purpose that he goo and zet down again.

GODLEIGH
Yu can't purpose that to this meetin'; yu can only purpose that to the old meetin' that's not zettin' any longer.

FREMAN [Excitedly]
I didn' care what old meetin' 'tis that's zettin'. I purpose that Sol Potter goo an' zet in that chair again, while I rise on my point of order.

TRUSTAFORD [Scratching his head]
'Tesn't regular but I guess yu've got to goo, Sol, or us shan't 'ave no peace.

[**SOL POTTER**, still wiping his brow, goes back to the chair.]

MORSE [Stolidly-to **FREMAN**]
Zet down, Will Freman.

[He pulls at him with a blacksmith's arm.]

FREMAN [Remaining erect with an effort]
I'm not a-goin' to zet down till I've arisen.

JARLAND
Now then, there 'e is in the chair. What's yore point of order?

FREMAN [Darting his eyes here and there, and flinging his hand up to his gipsy-like head]
'Twas—'twas—Darned ef y' 'aven't putt it clean out o' my 'ead.

JARLAND
We can't wait for yore points of order. Come out o' that chair. Sol Potter.

[**SOL POTTER** rises and is about to vacate the chair.]

FREMAN
I know! There ought to 'a been minutes taken. Yu can't 'ave no meetin' without minutes. When us comes to electin' a chairman o' the next meetin', 'e won't 'ave no minutes to read.

SOL POTTER
'Twas only to putt down that I was elected chairman to elect a meetin' to elect a chairman to preside over a meetin' to pass a resolution dalin' wi' the curate. That's aisy set down, that is.

FREMAN [Mollified]
We'll 'ave that zet down, then, while we're electin' the chairman o' the next meetin'.

[A silence.]

TRUSTAFORD
Well then, seein' this is the praaper old meetin' for carryin' the resolution about the curate, I purpose Mr. Sol Potter take the chair.

FREMAN
I purpose Mr. Trustaford. I 'aven't a-got nothin' against Sol Potter, but seein' that he elected the meetin' that's to elect 'im, it might be said that 'e was electin' of himzelf in a manner of spakin'. Us don't want that said.

MORSE [Amid meditative grunts from the dumb-as-fishes]
There's some-at in that. One o' they tu purposals must be putt to the meetin'.

FREMAN
Second must be putt virst, fur zure.

TRUSTAFORD
I dunno as I wants to zet in that chair. To hiss the curate, 'tis a ticklish sort of a job after that. Vurst comes afore second, Will Freeman.

FREMAN
Second is amendment to virst. 'Tes the amendments is putt virst.

TRUSTAFORD
'Ow's that, Mr. Godleigh? I'm not particular eggzac'ly to a dilly zort of a point like that.

SOL POTTER [Scratching his, head]
'Tes a very nice point, for zure.

GODLEIGH
'Tes undoubtedly for the chairman to decide.

[**VOICE** from the dumb-as fishes: "But there ain't no chairman yet."]

JARLAND
Sol Potter's chairman.

FREMAN
No, 'e ain't.

MORSE
Yes, 'e is—'e's chairman till this second old meetin' gets on the go.

FREMAN
I deny that. What du yu say, Mr. Trustaford?

TRUSTAFORD
I can't 'ardly tell. It du zeem a darned long-sufferin' sort of a business altogether.

[A silence.]

MORSE [Slowly]
Tell 'ee what 'tis, us shan't du no gude like this.

GODLEIGH
'Tes for Mr. Freman or Mr. Trustaford, one or t'other to withdraw their motions.

TRUSTAFORD [After a pause, with cautious generosity]
I've no objections to withdrawin' mine, if Will Freman'll withdraw his'n.

FREMAN
I won't never be be'indhand. If Mr. Trustaford withdraws, I withdraws mine.

MORSE [With relief]
That's zensible. Putt the motion to the meetin'.

SOL POTTER
There ain't no motion left to putt.

[Silence of consternation.]

[In the confusion **JIM BERE** is seen to stand up.]

GODLEIGH
Jim Bere to spike. Silence for Jim!

VOICES
Aye! Silence for Jim!

SOL POTTER
Well, Jim?

JIM [Smiling and slow]
Nothin' duin'.

TRUSTAFORD
Bravo, Jim! Yu'm right. Best zense yet!

[Applause from the dumb-as-fishes.]

[With his smile brightening, **JIM** resumes his seat.]

SOL POTTER [Wiping his brow]
Du seem to me, gentlemen, seem' as we'm got into a bit of a tangle in a manner of spakin', 'twid be the most zimplest and vairest way to begin all over vrom the beginnin', so's t'ave it all vair an' square for every one.

[In the uproar Of "Aye" and "No," it is noticed that **TIBBY JARLAND** is standing in front of her father with her finger, for want of something better, in her mouth.]

TIBBY [In her stolid voice]
Please, sister Mercy says, curate 'ave got to "Lastly."

[**JARLAND** picks her up, and there is silence.]

An' please to come quick.

JARLAND
Come on, mates; quietly now!

[He goes out, and all begin to follow him.]

MORSE [Slowest, save for **SOL POTTER**]
'Tes rare lucky us was all agreed to hiss the curate afore us began the botherin' old meetin', or us widn' 'ardly 'ave 'ad time to settle what to du.

SOL POTTER [Scratching his head]
Aye, 'tes rare lucky; but I dunno if 'tes altogether reg'lar.

SCENE III

The village green before the churchyard and the yew-trees at the gate. Into the pitch dark under the yews, light comes out through the half-open church door. Figures are lurking, or moving stealthily—people waiting and listening to the sound of a voice speaking in the church words that are inaudible. Excited whispering and faint giggles come from the deepest yew-tree shade, made ghostly by the white faces and the frocks of young girls continually flitting up and back in the blackness. A girl's figure comes flying out from the porch, down the path of light, and joins the stealthy group.

WHISPERING VOICE of MERCY
Where's 'e got to now, Gladys?

WHISPERING VOICE OF GLADYS
'E've just finished.

VOICE OF CONNIE
Whu pushed t'door open?

VOICE OF GLADYS
Tim Clyst I giv' it a little push, meself.

VOICE OF CONNIE
Oh!

VOICE of GLADYS
Tim Clyst's gone in!

ANOTHER VOICE
O-o-o-h!

VOICE of MERCY
Whu else is there, tu?

VOICE OF GLADYS
Ivy's there, an' Old Mrs. Potter, an' tu o' the maids from th'Hall; that's all as ever.

VOICE of CONNIE
Not the old grey mare?

VOICE of GLADYS
No. She ain't ther'. 'Twill just be th'ymn now, an' the Blessin'. Tibby gone for 'em?

VOICE OF MERCY

Yes.

VOICE of CONNIE
Mr. Burlacombe's gone in home, I saw 'im pass by just now—'e don' like it. Father don't like it neither.

VOICE of MERCY
Mr. Strangway shoudn' 'ave taken my skylark, an' thrown father out o' winder. 'Tis goin' to be awful fun! Oh!

[She jumps up and dawn in the darkness. And a **VOICE** from far in the shadow says: "Hsssh! Quiet, yu maids!" The **VOICE** has ceased speaking in the church. There is a moment's dead silence. The **VOICE** speaks again; then from the wheezy little organ come the first faint chords of a hymn.]

GLADYS
"Nearer, my God, to Thee!"

VOICE of MERCY
'Twill be funny, with no one 'ardly singin'.

[The sound of the old hymn sung by just six **VOICES** comes out to them rather sweet and clear.]

GLADYS [Softly]
'Tis pretty, tu. Why! They're only singin' one verse!

[A moment's silence, and the **VOICE** speaks, uplifted, pronouncing the Blessing: "The peace of God—" As the last words die away, dark **FIGURES** from the inn approach over the grass, till quite a **CROWD** seems standing there without a word spoken. Then from out of the church porch come the congregation. **TIM CLYST** first, hastily lost among the waiting figures in the dark; old **MRS POTTER**, a half blind old lady groping her way and perceiving nothing out of the ordinary; the two maids from the Hall, self-conscious and scared, scuttling along. Last, **IVY BURLACOMBE** quickly, and starting back at the dim, half-hidden crowd.]

VOICE of GLADYS [Whispering]
Ivy! Here, quick!

[**IVY** sways, darts off towards the voice, and is lost in the shadow.]

VOICE OF FREMAN [Low]
Wait, boys, till I give signal.

[Two or three squirks and giggles; **TIM CLYST'S** voice: "Ya-as! Don't 'ee tread on my toe!" A soft, frightened "O-o-h!" from a **GIRL**. Some quick, excited whisperings: "Luke!" "Zee there!" "He's comin'!" And then a perfectly dead silence. The figure of **STRANGWAY** is seen in his dark clothes, passing from the vestry to the church porch. He stands plainly visible in the lighted porch, locking the door, then steps forward. Just as he reaches the edge of the porch, a low hiss breaks the silence. It swells very gradually into a long, hissing groan. **STRANGWAY** stands motionless, his hand over his eyes, staring into the darkness. A girl's **FIGURE** can be seen to break out of the darkness and rush away. When at last the groaning has died into sheer expectancy, **STRANGWAY** drops his hand.]

STRANGWAY [In a loco voice]
Yes! I'm glad. Is Jarland there?

FREMAN
He's 'ere-no thanks to yu! Hsss!

[The hiss breaks out again, then dies away.]

JARLAND'S VOICE [Threatening]
Try if yu can du it again.

STRANGWAY
No, Jarland, no! I ask you to forgive me. Humbly!

[A hesitating silence, broken by muttering.]

CLYST'S VOICE
Bravo!

A VOICE
That's vair.

A VOICE
'E's afraid o' the sack—that's what 'tis.

A VOICE [Groaning]
'E's a praaper coward.

A VOICE
Whu funked the doctor?

CLYST'S VOICE
Shame on 'ee, therr!

STRANGWAY
You're right—all of you! I'm not fit! An uneasy and excited mustering and whispering dies away into renewed silence.

STRANGWAY
What I did to Tam Jarland is not the real cause of what you're doing, is it? I understand. But don't be troubled. It's all over. I'm going—you'll get some one better. Forgive me, Jarland. I can't see your face—it's very dark.

FREMAN'S Voice [Mocking] Wait for the full mune.

GODLEIGH [Very low]
"My 'eart 'E lighted not!"

STRANGWAY [Starting at the sound of his own words thus mysteriously given him out of the darkness] Whoever found that, please tear it up!

[After a moment's silence]

Many of you have been very kind to me. You won't see me again—Good-bye, all!

[He stands for a second motionless, then moves resolutely down into the darkness so peopled with shadows.]

UNCERTAIN VOICES AS HE PASSES
Good-bye, zurr!
Good luck, zurr!

[He has gone.]

CLYST'S VOICE
Three cheers for Mr. Strangway!

[And a queer, strangled cheer, with groans still threading it, arises.]

ACT III

SCENE I

In the Burlacombe's' hall-sitting-room the curtains are drawn, a lamp burns, and the door stands open. **BURLACOMBE** and his **WIFE** are hovering there, listening to the sound of mingled cheers and groaning.

MRS BURLACOMBE
Aw! my gudeness—what a thing t'appen! I'd saner 'a lost all me ducks.

[She makes towards the inner door]

I can't never face 'im.

BURLACOMBE
'E can't expect nothin' else, if 'e act like that.

MRS BURLACOMBE
'Tes only duin' as 'e'd be done by.

BURLACOMBE
Aw! Yu can't go on forgivin' 'ere, an' forgivin' there. 'Tesn't nat'ral.

MRS BURLACOMBE

'Tes the mischief 'e'm a parson. 'Tes 'im bein' a lamb o' God—or 'twidden be so quare for 'im to be forgivin'.

BURLACOMBE
Yu goo an' make un a gude 'ot drink.

MRS BURLACOMBE
Poor soul! What'll 'e du now, I wonder? [Under her breath] 'E's cumin'!

[She goes hurriedly. **BURLACOMBE**, with a startled look back, wavers and makes to follow her, but stops undecided in the inner doorway. **STRANGWAY** comes in from the darkness. He turns to the window and drops overcoat and hat and the church key on the windowseat, looking about him as men do when too hard driven, and never fixing his eyes long enough on anything to see it. **BURLACOMBE**, closing the door into the house, advances a step. At the sound **STRANGWAY** faces round.]

BURLACOMBE
I wanted for yu to know, zurr, that me an' mine 'adn't nothin' to du wi' that darned fulishness, just now.

STRANGWAY [With a ghost of a smile]
Thank you, Burlacombe. It doesn't matter. It doesn't matter a bit.

BURLACOMBE
I 'ope yu won't take no notice of it. Like a lot o' silly bees they get. [After an uneasy pause] Yu'll excuse me spakin' of this mornin', an' what 'appened. 'Tes a brave pity it cam' on yu so sudden-like before yu 'ad time to think. 'Tes a sort o' thing a man shude zet an' chew upon. Certainly 'tes not a bit o' yuse goin' against human nature. Ef yu don't stand up for yureself there's no one else not goin' to. 'Tes yure not 'avin' done that 'as made 'em so rampageous. [Stealing another look at **STRANGWAY**] Yu'll excuse me, zurr, spakin' of it, but 'tes amazin' sad to zee a man let go his own, without a word o' darin'. 'Tea as ef 'e 'ad no passions like.

STRANGWAY
Look at me, Burlacombe.

[**BURLACOMBE** looks up, trying hard to keep his eyes on **STRANGWAY'S**, that seem to burn in his thin face.]

STRANGWAY
Do I look like that? Please, please!

[He touches his breast]

I've too much here. Please!

BURLACOMBE [With a sort of startled respect]
Well, zurr, 'tes not for me to zay nothin', certainly.

[He turns and after a slow look back at **STRANGWAY** goes out.]

STRANGWAY [To himself]
Passions! No passions! Ha!

[The outer door is opened and **IVY BURLACOMBE** appears, and, seeing him, stops. Then, coming softly towards him, she speaks timidly.]

IVY
Oh! Mr. Strangway, Mrs. Bradmere's cumin' from the Rectory. I ran an' told 'em. Oh! 'twas awful.

[**STRANGWAY** starts, stares at her, and turning on his heel, goes into the house. **IVY'S** face is all puckered, as if she were on the point of tears. There is a gentle scratching at the door, which has not been quite closed.]

VOICE OF GLADYS [Whispering]
Ivy! Come on Ivy. I won't.

VOICE OF MERCY
Yu must. Us can't du without Yu.

IVY [Going to the door]
I don't want to.

VOICE of GLADYS
"Naughty maid, she won't come out," Ah! du 'ee!

VOICE OF CREMER
Tim Clyst an' Bobbie's cumin'; us'll only be six anyway. Us can't dance "figure of eight" without yu.

IVY [Stamping her foot]
I don't want to dance at all! I don't.

MERCY
Aw! She's temper. Yu can bang on tambourine, then!

GLADYS [Running in]
Quick, Ivy! Here's the old grey mare cumin' down the green. Quick.

[With whispering and scuffling; gurgling and squeaking, the reluctant **IVY'S** hand is caught and she is jerked away. In their haste they have left the door open behind them.]

VOICE of MRS BRADMERE [Outside]
Who's that?

[She knocks loudly, and rings a bell; then, without waiting, comes in through the open door.]

[Noting the overcoat and hat on the window-sill she moves across to ring the bell. But as she does so, **MRS BURLACOMBE**, followed by **BURLACOMBE**, comes in from the house.]

MRS BRADMERE

This disgraceful business! Where's Mr. Strangway? I see he's in.

MRS BURLACOMBE

Yes, m'm, he'm in—but—but Burlacombe du zay he'm terrible upset.

MRS BRADMERE

I should think so. I must see him—at once.

MRS BURLACOMBE

I doubt bed's the best place for 'un, an' gude 'ot drink. Burlacombe zays he'm like a man standin' on the edge of a cliff; and the lasts tipsy o' wind might throw un over.

MRS BRADMERE [To **BURLACOMBE**]

You've seen him, then?

BURLACOMBE

Yeas; an' I don't like the luke of un—not a little bit, I don't.

MRS BURLACOMBE [Almost to herself]

Poor soul; 'e've a-'ad to much to try un this yer long time past. I've a-seen 'tis sperrit cumin' thru 'is body, as yu might zay. He's torn to bits, that's what 'tis.

BURLACOMBE

'Twas a praaper cowardly thing to hiss a man when he's down. But 'twas natural tu, in a manner of spakin'. But 'tesn't that troublin' 'im. 'Tes in here [touching his forehead], along of his wife, to my thinkin'. They zay 'e've a-known about 'er a-fore she went away. Think of what 'e've 'ad to kape in all this time. 'Tes enough to drive a man silly after that. I've a-locked my gun up. I see a man like—like that once before—an' sure enough 'e was dead in the mornin'!

MRS BRADMERE

Nonsense, Burlacombe! [To **MRS BURLACOMBE**] Go and
tell him I want to see him—must see him.

[**MRS BURLACOMBE** goes into the house]

And look here, Burlacombe; if we catch any one, man or woman, talking of this outside the village, it'll be the end of their tenancy, whoever they may be. Let them all know that. I'm glad he threw that drunken fellow out of the window, though it was a little—

BURLACOMBE

Aye! The nuspapers would be praaper glad of that, for a tiddy bit o' nuse.

MRS BRADMERE

My goodness! Yes! The men are all up at the inn. Go and tell them what I said—it's not to get about. Go at once, Burlacombe.

BURLACOMBE

Must be a turrable job for 'im, every one's knowin' about 'is wife like this. He'm a proud man tu, I think. 'Tes a funny business altogether!

MRS BRADMERE
Horrible! Poor fellow! Now, come! Do your best, Burlacombe!

[**BURLACOMBE** touches his forelock and goes. **MRS BRADMERE** stands quite still, thinking. Then going to the photograph, she stares up at it.]

MRS BRADMERE
You baggage!

[**STRANGWAY** has come in noiselessly, and is standing just behind her. She turns, and sees him. There is something so still, so startlingly still in his figure and white face, that she cannot for the moment fond her voice.]

MRS BRADMERE [At last]
This is most distressing. I'm deeply sorry.

[Then, as he does not answer, she goes a step closer]

I'm an old woman; and old women must take liberties, you know, or they couldn't get on at all. Come now! Let's try and talk it over calmly and see if we can't put things right.

STRANGWAY
You were very good to come; but I would rather not.

MRS BRADMERE
I know you're in as grievous trouble as a man can be.

STRANGWAY
Yes.

MRS BRADMERE [With a little sound of sympathy]
What are you—thirty-five? I'm sixty-eight if I'm a day—old enough to be your mother. I can feel what you must have been through all these months, I can indeed. But you know you've gone the wrong way to work. We aren't angels down here below! And a son of the Church can't act as if for himself alone. The eyes of every one are on him.

STRANGWAY [Taking the church key from the window.]
Take this, please.

MRS BRADMERE
No, no, no! Jarland deserved all he got. You had great provocation.

STRANGWAY
It's not Jarland.

[Holding out the key]

Please take it to the Rector. I beg his forgiveness.

[Touching his breast]

There's too much I can't speak of—can't make plain. Take it to him, please.

MRS BRADMERE
Mr. Strangway—I don't accept this. I am sure my husband—the Church—will never accept—

STRANGWAY
Take it!

MRS BRADMERE [Almost unconsciously taking it]
Mind! We don't accept it. You must come and talk to the Rector to-morrow. You're overwrought. You'll see it all in another light, then.

STRANGWAY [With a strange smile]
Perhaps.

[Lifting the blind]

Beautiful night! Couldn't be more beautiful!

MRS BRADMERE [Startled-softly]
Don't turn sway from these who want to help you! I'm a grumpy old woman, but I can feel for you. Don't try and keep it all back, like this! A woman would cry, and it would all seem clearer at once. Now won't you let me—?

STRANGWAY
No one can help, thank you.

MRS BRADMERE
Come! Things haven't gone beyond mending, really, if you'll face them.

[Pointing to the photograph]

You know what I mean. We dare not foster immorality.

STRANGWAY [Quivering as at a jabbed nerve]
Don't speak of that!

MRS BRADMERE
But think what you've done, Mr. Strangway! If you can't take your wife back, surely you must divorce her. You can never help her to go on like this in secret sin.

STRANGWAY

Torture her—one way or the other?

MRS BRADMERE
No, no; I want you to do as the Church—as all Christian society would wish. Come! You can't let this go on. My dear man, do your duty at all costs!

STRANGWAY
Break her heart?

MRS BRADMERE
Then you love that woman—more than God!

STRANGWAY [His face quivering]
Love!

MRS BRADMERE
They told me—Yes, and I can see you're is a bad way. Come, pull yourself together! You can't defend what you're doing.

STRANGWAY
I do not try.

MRS BRADMERE
I must get you to see! My father was a clergyman; I'm married to one; I've two sons in the Church. I know what I'm talking about. It's a priest's business to guide the people's lives.

STRANGWAY [Very low]
But not mine! No more!

MRS BRADMERE [Looking at him shrewdly]
There's something very queer about you to-night. You ought to see doctor.

STRANGWAY [A smile awning and going on his lips]
If I am not better soon—

MRS BRADMERE
I know it must be terrible to feel that everybody—

[A convulsive shiver passes over **STRANGWAY**, and he shrinks against the door]

But come! Live it down!

[With anger growing at his silence]

Live it down, man! You can't desert your post—and let these villagers do what they like with us? Do you realize that you're letting a woman, who has treated you abominably;—yes, abominably —go scot-free, to live comfortably with another man? What an example!

STRANGWAY
Will you, please, not speak of that!

MRS BRADMERE
I must! This great Church of ours is based on the rightful condemnation of wrongdoing. There are times when forgiveness is a sin, Michael Strangway. You must keep the whip hand. You must fight!

STRANGWAY
Fight!

[Touching his heart]

My fight is here. Have you ever been in hell? For months and months—burned and longed; hoped against hope; killed a man in thought day by day? Never rested, for love and hate? I—condemn! I—judge! No! It's rest I have to find—somewhere—somehow-rest! And how—how can I find rest?

MRS BRADMERE [Who has listened to his outburst in a soft of coma]
You are a strange man! One of these days you'll go off your head if you don't take care.

STRANGWAY [Smiling]
One of these days the flowers will grow out of me; and I shall sleep.

[**MRS BRADMERE** stares at his smiling face a long moment in silence, then with a little sound, half sniff, half snort, she goes to the door. There she halts.]

MRS BRADMERE
And you mean to let all this go on—Your wife—

STRANGWAY
Go! Please go!

MRS BRADMERE
Men like you have been buried at cross-roads before now! Take care! God punishes!

STRANGWAY
Is there a God?

MRS BRADMERE
Ah! [With finality] You must see a doctor.

[Seeing that the look on his face does not change, she opens the door, and hurries away into the moonlight.]

[**STRANGWAY** crosses the room to where his wife's picture hangs, and stands before it, his hands grasping the frame. Then he takes it from the wall, and lays it face upwards on the window seat.]

STRANGWAY [To himself]
Gone! What is there, now?

[The sound of an owl's hooting is floating in, and of voices from the green outside the inn.]

STRANGWAY [To himself]
Gone! Taken faith—hope—life!

[**JIM BERE** comes wandering into the open doorway.]

JIM BERE
Gude avenin', zurr.

[At his slow gait, with his feeble smile, he comes in, and standing by the window-seat beside the long dark coat that still lies there, he looks down at **STRANGWAY** with his lost eyes.]

JIM
Yu threw un out of winder. I cud 'ave, once, I cud.

[**STRANGWAY** neither moves nor speaks; and **JIM BERE** goes on with his unimaginably slow speech]

They'm laughin' at yu, zurr. An' so I come to tell 'ee how to du. 'Twas full mune—when I caught 'em, him an' my girl. I caught 'em.

[With a strange and awful flash of fire]

—I did; an' I tuk un—

[He's taken up **STRANGWAY'S** coat and grips it with his trembling hands, as a man grips another's neck]

—like that—I tuk un.

[As the coat falls, like a body out of which the breath has been squeezed, **STRANGWAY**, rising, catches it.]

STRANGWAY [Gripping the coat]
And he fell!

[He lets the coat fall on the floor, and puts his foot on it. Then, staggering back, he leans against the window.]

JIM
Yu see, I loved 'er—I did.

[The lost look comes back to his eyes]

Then somethin'—I dunno—and—and—

[He lifts his hand and passes it up and down his side]

Twas like this for ever.

[They gaze at each other in silence.]

JIM [At last]
I come to tell yu. They'm all laughin' at yu. But yu'm strong—yu go over to Durford to that doctor man, an' take un like I did. [He tries again to make the sign of squeezing a man's neck] They can't laugh at yu no more, then. Tha's what I come to tell yu. Tha's the way for a Christian man to du. Gude naight, zurr. I come to tell yee.

[**STRANGWAY** motions to him in silence. And, very slowly, **JIM BERE** passes out.]

[The voices of **MEN** coming down the green are heard.]

VOICES
Gude night, Tam. Glide naight, old Jim!

VOICES
Gude might, Mr. Trustaford. 'Tes a wonderful fine mune.

VOICE OF TRUSTAFORD
Ah! 'Tes a brave mune for th' poor old curate!

VOICE
"My 'eart 'E lighted not!"

[**TRUSTAFORD'S** laugh, and the rattling, fainter and fainter, of wheels. A spasm seizes on **STRANGWAY'S** face, as he stands there by the open door, his hand grips his throat; he looks from side to side, as if seeking a way of escape.]

SCENE II

The Burlacombe's high and nearly empty barn. A lantern is hung by a rope that lifts the bales of straw, to a long ladder leaning against a rafter. This gives all the light there is, save for a slender track of moonlight, slanting in from the end, where the two great doors are not quite closed. On a rude bench in front of a few remaining, stacked, square-cut bundles of last year's hay, sits **TIBBY JARLAND**, a bit of apple in her mouth, sleepily beating on a tambourine. With stockinged feet **GLADYS, IVY, CONNIE,** and **MERCY, TIM CLYST,** and **BOBBIE JARLAND**, a boy of fifteen, are dancing a truncated "Figure of Eight"; and their shadow are dancing alongside on the walls. Shoes and some apples have been thrown down close to the side door through which they have come in. Now and then **IVY**, the smallest and best of the dancers, ejaculates words of direction, and one of the youths grunts or breathes loudly out of the confusion of his mind. Save for this and the dumb beat and jingle of the sleepy tambourine, there is no sound. The dance comes to its end, but the drowsy **TIBBY** goes on beating.

MERCY
That'll du, Tibby; we're finished. Ate yore apple.

[The stolid **TIBBY** eats her apple.]

CLYST [In his teasing, excitable voice]
Yu maids don't dance 'elf's well as us du. Bobbie 'e's a great dancer. 'E dance vine. I'm a gude dancer, meself.

GLADYS
A'n't yu conceited just?

CLYST
Aw! Ah! Yu'll give me kiss for that.

[He chases, but cannot catch that slippery white figure]

Can't she glimmer!

MERCY
Gladys! Up ladder!

CLYST
Yu go up ladder; I'll catch 'ee then. Naw, yu maids, don't yu give her succour. That's not vair

[Catching hold of **MERCY**, who gives a little squeal.]

CONNIE
Mercy, don't! Mrs. Burlacombe'll hear. Ivy, go an' peek.

[**IVY** goes to flee side door and peers through.]

CLYST [Abandoning the chase and picking up an apple—they all have the joyous irresponsibility that attends forbidden doings]
Ya-as, this is a gude apple. Luke at Tibby!

[**TIBBY**, overcome by drowsiness, has fallen back into the hay, asleep. **GLADYS**, leaning against the hay breaks into humming:]

"There cam' three dukes a-ridin', a-ridin', a-ridin',
There cam' three dukes a ridin'
With a ransy-tansy tay!"

CLYST
Us 'as got on vine; us'll get prize for our dancin'.

CONNIE
There won't be no prize if Mr. Strangway goes away. 'Tes funny 'twas Mrs. Strangway start us.

IVY [From the door]

'Twas wicked to hiss him.

[A moment's hush.]

CLYST
Twasn't I.

BOBBIE
I never did.

GLADYS
Oh! Bobbie, yu did! Yu blew in my ear.

CLYST
'Twas the praaper old wind in the trees. Did make a brave noise, zurely.

MERCY
'E shuld'n' 'a let my skylark go.

CLYST
[Out of sheer contradictoriness] Ya-as, 'e shude, then.
What du yu want with th' birds of the air? They'm no gude to yu.

IVY [Mournfully]
And now he's goin' away.

CLYST
Ya-as; 'tes a pity. He's the best man I ever seen since I was comin' from my mother. He's a gude man.
He'em got a zad face, sure enough, though.

IVY
Gude folk always 'ave zad faces.

CLYST
I knu a gude man—'e sold pigs—very gude man: 'e 'ad a budiful bright vase like the mane.

[Touching his stomach]

I was sad, meself, once. 'Twas a funny scrabblin'—like feelin'.

GLADYS
If 'e go away, whu's goin' to finish us for confirmation?

CONNIE
The Rector and the old grey mare.

MERCY
I don' want no more finishin'; I'm confirmed enough.

CLYST
Ya-as; yu'm a buty.

GLADYS
Suppose we all went an' asked 'im not to go?

IVY
'Twouldn't be no gude.

CONNIE
Where's 'e goin'?

MERCY
He'll go to London, of course.

IVY
He's so gentle; I think 'e'll go to an island, where there's nothin' but birds and beasts and flowers.

CLYST
Aye! He'm awful fond o' the dumb things.

IVY
They're kind and peaceful; that's why.

CLYST
Aw! Yu see tu praaper old tom cats; they'm not to peaceful, after that, nor kind naighther.

BOBBIE [Surprisingly]
If 'e's sad, per'aps 'e'll go to 'Eaven.

IVY
Oh! not yet, Bobbie. He's tu young.

CLYST [Following his own thoughts]
Ya-as. 'Tes a funny place, tu, nowadays, judgin' from the papers.

GLADYS
Wonder if there's dancin' in 'Eaven?

IVY
There's beasts, and flowers, and waters, and 'e told us.

CLYST
Naw! There's no dumb things in 'Eaven. Jim Bere 'e says there is! 'E thinks 'is old cat's there.

IVY

Yes. [Dreamily] There's stars, an' owls, an' a man playin' on the flute. Where 'tes gude, there must be music.

CLYST
Old brass band, shuldn' wonder, like th' Salvation Army.

IVY [Putting up her hands to an imaginary pipe]
No; 'tis a boy that goes so; an' all the dumb things an' all the people goo after 'im—like this.

[She marches slowly, playing her imaginary pipe, and one by one they all fall in behind her, padding round the barn in their stockinged feet. Passing the big doors, **IVY** throws them open.]

An' 'tes all like that in 'Eaven.

[She stands there gazing out, still playing on her imaginary pipe. And they all stand a moment silent, staring into the moonlight.]

CLYST
'Tes a glory-be full mune to-night!

IVY
A goldie-cup—a big one. An' millions o' little goldie-cups on the floor of 'Eaven.

MERCY
Oh! Bother 'Eaven! Let's dance "Clapperclaws"! Wake up, Tibby!

GLADYS
Clapperelaws, clapperclaws! Come on, Bobbie—make circle!

CLYST
Clapperclaws! I dance that one fine.

IVY [Taking the tambourine]
See, Tibby; like this. She hums and beats gently, then restores the tambourine to the sleepy **TIBBY**, who, waking, has placed a piece of apple in her mouth.

CONNIE
'Tes awful difficult, this one.

IVY [Illustrating]
No; yu just jump, an' clap yore 'ands. Lovely, lovely!

CLYST
Like ringin' bells! Come ahn!

[**TIBBY** begins her drowsy beating, **IVY** hums the tune; they dance, and their shadows dance again upon the walls. When she has beaten but a few moments on the tambourine, **TIBBY** is overcome once more by sleep and falls back again into her nest of hay, with her little shoed feet just visible over the edge of the bench. **IVY** catches up the tambourine, and to her beating and humming the dancers dance on.]

[Suddenly **GLADYS** stops like a wild animal surprised, and cranes her neck towards the aide door.]

CONNIE [Whispering]
What is it?

GLADYS [Whispering]
I hear—some one comin' across the yard.

[She leads a noiseless scamper towards the shoes. **BOBBIE JARLAND** shins up the ladder and seizes the lantern. **IVY** drops the tambourine. They all fly to the big doors, and vanish into the moonlight, pulling the door nearly to again after them.]

[There is the sound of scrabbling at the hitch of the side door, and **STRANGWAY** comes into the nearly dark barn. Out in the night the owl is still hooting. He closes the door, and that sound is lost. Like a man walking in his sleep, he goes up to the ladder, takes the rope in his hand, and makes a noose. He can be heard breathing, and in the darkness the motions of his hands are dimly seen, freeing his throat and putting the noose round his neck. He stands swaying to and fro at the foot of the ladder; then, with a sigh, sets his foot on it to mount. One of the big doors creaks and opens in the wind, letting in a broad path of moonlight.]

[**STRANGWAY** stops; freeing his neck from the noose, he walks quickly up the track of moonlight, whitened from head to foot, to close the doors.]

[The sound of his boots on the bare floor has awakened **TIBBY JARLAND** Struggling out of her hay nest she stands staring at his whitened figure, and bursts suddenly into a wail.]

TIBBY
O-oh! Mercy! Where are yu? I'm frightened! I'm frightened! O-oooo!

STRANGWAY [Turning—startled]
Who's that? Who is it?

TIBBY
O-oh! A ghosty! Oo-ooo!

STRANGWAY [Going to her quickly]
It's me, Tibby—Tib only me!

TIBBY
I seed a ghosty.

STRANGWAY [Taking her up]
No, no, my bird, you didn't! It was me.

TIBBY [Burying her face against him]

I'm frighted. It was a big one. [She gives tongue again] O-o-oh!

STRANGWAY
There, there! It's nothing but me. Look!

TIBBY
No.

[She peeps out all the same.]

STRANGWAY
See! It's the moonlight made me all white. See! You're a brave girl now?

TIBBY [Cautiously]
I want my apple.

[She points towards her nest. **STRANGWAY** carries her there, picks up an apple, and gives it her. **TIBBY** takes a bite.]

TIBBY
I want any tambourine.

STRANGWAY [Giving her the tambourine, and carrying her back into the' track of moonlight]
Now we're both ghosties! Isn't it funny?

TIBBY. [Doubtfully]
Yes.

STRANGWAY
See! The moon's laughing at us! See? Laugh then!

[**TIBBY**, tambourine in one hand and apple in the other, smiles stolidly. He sets her down on the ladder, and stands, holding her level With him.]

TIBBY [Solemnly]
I'se still frightened.

STRANGWAY
No! Full moon, Tibby! Shall we wish for it?

TABBY
Full mune.

STRANGWAY
Moon! We're wishing for you. Moon, moon!

TIBBY
Mune, we're wishin' for yu!

STRANGWAY
What do, you wish it to be?

TIBBY
Bright new shillin'!

STRANGWAY
A face.

TIBBY
Shillin', a shillin'!

STRANGWAY [Taking out a shilling and spinning it so that it falls into her pinafore]
See! Your wish comes true.

TIBBY
Oh!

[Putting the shilling in her mouth]

Mune's still there!

STRANGWAY
Wish for me, Tibby!

TIBBY
Mune. I'm wishin' for yu!

STRANGWAY
Not yet!

TIBBY
Shall I shake my tambouline?

STRANGWAY
Yes, shake your tambouline.

TIBBY [Shaking her tambourine]
Mune, I'm shaken' at yu.

[**STRANGWAY** lays his hand suddenly on the rope, and swings it up on to the beam.]

TIBBY
What d'yu du that for?

STRANGWAY
To put it out of reach. It's better—

TIBBY
Why is it better?

[She stares up at him.]

STRANGWAY
Come along, Tibby!

[He carries her to the big doors, and sets her down]

See! All asleep! The birds, and the fields, and the moon!

TIBBY
Mune, mune, we're wishing for yu!

STRANGWAY
Send her your love, and say good-night.

TIBBY [Blowing a kiss]
Good-night, mune!

[From the barn roof a little white dove's feather comes floating down in the wind. **TIBBY** follows it with her hand, catches it, and holds it up to him.]

TIBBY [Chuckling]
Luke. The mune's sent a bit o' love!

STRANGWAY [Taking the feather]
Thank you, Tibby! I want that bit o' love.

[Very faint, comes the sound of music]

Listen!

TIBBY
It's Miss Willis, playin' on the pianny!

STRANGWAY
No; it's Love; walking and talking in the world.

TIBBY
[Dubiously] Is it?

STRANGWAY [Pointing]
See! Everything coming out to listen! See them, Tibby! All the little things with pointed ears, children, and birds, and flowers, and bunnies; and the bright rocks, and—men! Hear their hearts beating! And the wind listening!

TIBBY
I can't hear—nor I can't see!

STRANGWAY
Beyond—[To himself] They are—they must be; I swear they are!

[Then, catching sight of **TIBBY'S** amazed eyes]

And now say good-bye to me.

TIBBY
Where yu goin'?

STRANGWAY
I don't know, Tibby.

VOICE OF MERCY [Distant and cautious]
Tibby! Tibby! Where are yu?

STRANGWAY
Mercy calling; run to her!

[**TIBBY** starts off, turns back and lifts her face. He bends to kiss her, and flinging her arms round his neck, she gives him a good hug. Then, knuckling the sleep out of her eyes, she runs.]

[**STRANGWAY** stands, uncertain. There is a sound of heavy footsteps; a **MAN** clears his throat, close by.]

STRANGWAY
Who's that?

CREMER
Jack Cremer.

[The big man's **FIGURE** appears out of the shadow of the barn]

That yu, zurr?

STRANGWAY
Yes, Jack. How goes it?

CREMER
'Tes empty, zurr. But I'll get on some'ow.

STRANGWAY
You put me to shame.

CREMER

No, zurr. I'd be killin' meself, if I didn' feel I must stick it, like yu zaid.

[They stand gazing at each other in the moonlight.

STRANGWAY [Very low]
I honour you.

CREMER
What's that?

[Then, as **STRANGWAY** does not answer]

I'll just be walkin'—I won' be gain' 'ome to-night. 'Tes the full mune—lucky.

STRANGWAY [Suddenly]
Wait for me at the crossroads, Jack. I'll come with you. Will you have me, brother?

CREMER
Sure!

STRANGWAY
Wait, then.

CREMER
Aye, zurr.

[With his heavy tread **CREMER** passes on. And **STRANGWAY** leans against the lintel of the door, looking at the moon, that, quite full and golden, hangs not far above the straight horizon, where the trees stand small, in a row.

STRANGWAY [Lifting his hand in the gesture of prayer]
God, of the moon and the sun; of joy and beauty, of loneliness and sorrow—give me strength to go on, till I love every living thing!

[He moves away, following **JACK CREMER.** The full moon shines; the owl hoots; and some one is shaking **TIBBY'S** tambourine.

John Galsworthy – A Short Biography

John Galsworthy, eldest son of John Galsworthy (1817-1904), a solicitor and company director of Old Jewry, London, and Blanche Bailey (1835-1915), daughter of Charles Bartleet, a needlemaker in Redditch. His father's ancestors originated in Wembury, near Plymouth in England, and Galsworthy, for whom family origins were of significant importance, maintained a close connection with Devon. His more immediate family were considerably wealthy and well established in the shipping industry, and owned a fine estate in Kingston-upon-Thames called Parkfield, where Galsworthy was born on the 14th August 1867. At the age of nine he began education at Saugeen, a Bournemouth preparatory school, before starting at Harrow school in 1881 where he remained until 1886, distinguishing himself as an athlete.

His education at Harrow being successful enough to gain him entrance to Oxford, he began at New College to read law and gained a second-class degree with honours in 1889. Following Lincoln's Inn he was called to the bar in 1890. Despite this recognition he realised that he was not keen to actually begin practising law and so he resolved instead to look after the family's shipping business while specialising himself in Marine Law. This decision saw him take to the seas to destinations such as Vancouver, Island and South AFrica, though it was at the age of twenty-five on one particular journey to Australia, motivated by an (unfulfilled) intention to meet Robert Louis Stevenson on Samoa that he would being to realise fully his literary interests: though he was not considering becoming a writer at this time, his enjoyment of literature was enough to encourage an attempt at meeting a great writer and eventually enabled one of the most significant encounters of his life. He made the journey with his friend Edward Sanderson and, though he missed Stevenson, he met Joseph Conrad, a fellow future author famed for his novels which were often nautically themed. At the time Conrad was the first mate of the sailing-ship Torrens moored in the harbour of Adelaide, Australia; still very much focused on his ship-borne career, he was yet to begin his writing in earnest.

Indeed, though neither knew at the time, both Conrad and Galsworthy were at similar junctures in their lives, their time spent as sea acting as a transitional period during which each found their literary calling. It is perhaps owning to this unknown common ground that they became close friends. During his time on the Torrens Galsworthy recorded several details, offering a frank and valuable characterisation of Conrad while also illuminating his own experiences as a student of Marine Law.

> "I supposed to be studying navigation for the Admiralty Bar, would every day work out the position of the ship with the captain. On one side of the saloon table we would sit and check our observations with those of Conrad, who from the other side of the table would look at us a little quizzically."

On his return to England and the cessation of his nautical voyaging, Galsworthy began an affair with the wife of his first cousin, Major Arthur John Galsworthy. Ada Nemesis Pearson Cooper (1864-1956), the daughter of Emanuel Copper, an obstetrician from Norwich, remained married to the Major for ten years and the affair remained secret for its duration. In order to conceal the affair they took considerable pains to avoid suspicion. One such tactic was to stay in a secluded farmhouse called Wingstone in the village on Manaton on Dartmoor, in Devon. In Galsworthy's decision to choose Devon as the location for their clandestine rendezvous we see evidence of Galsworthy's affection for the place of his father's origin. It was only when, in 1905, she divorced the Major that their affair became known following their marriage on 23rd September of that year.

Galsworthy now took to writing sometime after having met Conrad and his career began in earnest when, in 1897, his first work, From the Four Winds, a volume of short stories, was published under the pseudonym John Sinjohn. He succeeded this in 1898 with Jocelyn, his first novel, and then his second in 1900, Villa Rubein. In 1901 he published a second volume of short stories, A Man of Devon, which was the last of his work to be published under pseudonym. The first of his work to be published under his own name was The Island Pharisees in 1904, a novel of social observation, seasoned with flashes of satire and propaganda. His decision to write under his own name is arguably owing to the recent death of his father, either as a mark of respect to his name or because now he was able to publish freely without incurring the possibility of paternal disappointment at his choice of career. It also marked a shift in his professionalism; he had hitherto published with small, independent publishers, but The Island Pharisees was published by Heinemann, a far more established House and one with whom he remained for the duration of his writing career.

He arguably cemented his position and maturity as a writer when, in 1906, he saw the publication of both his first major play, The Silver Box, and the novel The Man of Property. Each was published to considerable critical acclaim, and to achieve both in such a short space of time was impressive. the Silver Box concerns the imbalance in the justice system with regards to criminals of differing class by contrasting the treatment of a poor thief and a rich thief, both of whom stole silver cigarette cases but for very different reasons. The complexity of individual experience when not dealt with in public is highlighted and questioned in a bravely critical manner; despite the clear issues it raises with class and privilege, the final night was attended by the Price and Princess of Wales. The Man of Property was the first novel in the famous The Forsyte Saga, a trilogy of novels with an 'interlude' between each one, written between 1906 and 1921. Dealing with the questions of status, class and materialism, The Man of Property introduces us to the Forsyte family, particularly Soames Forsyte, who is acutely aware of his status as 'new money' and equally keen to assert himself as a wealthy man. Jealous of his wife and desperate to own things in order to confirm his wealth to those observing him, he engineers a plan to keep his wife from her friends which backfires spectacularly when, instead of cutting her off, all Soames achieves is enabling her to have an affair. This drives Soames to terrible actions with terrible consequences, which Galsworthy depicts with confidence.

Very typically Edwardian, the novel focuses on conflict between property and art, and to a certain degree much of its emotional power is drawn from Galsworthy's own life, particularly his affair with Ada. Their rendezvous in the countryside of Devon mirror the manner in which Forsyte seeks to relocate his wife and; though theirs was a much healthier relationship, there are clear similarities. By examining the fragile nature of the class system and those moving within it Galsworthy offered an important perspective on the relationships between material wealth, personal happiness and obsession, and the manner in which these change over time. His contemporaries widely regarded the publication of this novel as marking the end of Victorianism. His friend Conrad praised it as "indubitably a piece of art" and, though the notoriously risqué D.H. Lawrence lamented the novel's timidity in the face of sexuality and sensuality, he considered it potentially "a very great novel, a very great satire".

Though he continued to write both plays and novels, it was his work as a playwright for which he was most celebrated by his contemporaries. Indeed, his next novel, The Country House, seems uncharacteristically unfocused, its satirical view of those belonging to the country set comparatively unremarkable and weakly characterised, while at times the tone of satire becomes one of ironic detachment. In 1909 he published Fraternity, an exploration of of the various connections between urban society and the social classes therein, though its representation of lower-class Londoners is utterly unconvincing and ill-informed. Remaining with the subject of the landed gentry and the society surrounding it, in 1915 he published The Freelands, which does not stray far from conservative discussions of capitalism, the rural economy and their interrelationship.

His drama, however, featured a convincingly muted realism, directed at a relatively small, educated and politically-aware audience. His social agenda is prevalent here too, and is represented in a simple and static manner producing arresting instances of high drama. This talent for creating moments of captivating theatre is complimented by an instinctual sense of balance enabling his narratives to vacillate between their emotional high- and low-points, ultimately reaching conclusive equilibrium. This is particularly evident in one of his most popular plays, Strife, published in 1909 and examining the antagonists in a strike at a Cornish tin mine. In this, and in 1910's Justice, he approaches his subject with sympathy, irony and balance, which establishes a position of narrative authority while garnering the audiences trust that he is representing his characters and their motives justly. Justice condemns the use of solitary confinement in prisons, a reformist agenda which caught the liberality of his contemporary audiences along with the home secretary, Winston Churchill. Despite he was careful to disassociate himself with politics and professed himself apolitical, he and his work were nevertheless aligned with the views of the Liberal establishment. He spent much of the duration of the First World War working in a field hospital in France as an orderly having been passed over for military service.

Despite the popularity and brilliance of his work, it was only in 1920 that he had his first true commercial success with The Skin Game, a melodrama dealing with ethics, property and class. The play was adapted by Alfred Hitchcock in 1931. Galsworthy, meanwhile, had turned down a knighthood in 1918, considering his work not sufficient to be made a knight of the realm. He did, however, accept the Belgian Palmes d'Or in the following year. In 1920 he published the second novel in the Forsyte Saga, In Chancery, in which he resumes many of the themes of the first novel, focusing on the marital disharmony between Soames Forsyte and his wife. Katherine Mansfield considered it "a fascinating, brilliant book" in her review in The Atheneum. Then, in 1921, he was elected as the PEN International Literary Club's first president. The concluding novel to The Forsyte Saga, To Let was published in 1921 with a kind of peace being found between Forsyte and his now-ex wife, though he is left contemplating his losses and his greed. More ironic treatment of class confusions followed in Loyalties, bringing with it more popular success which lasted until 1926 and Escape, the last of his popular plays. Though he enjoyed popular success it was inconsistent and relatively small. His Collected Plays was published in 1929.

Over the course of time the appreciation of his work has gradually shifted from his plays to his novels, and particularly the detail and intricacy of his chronicle of English social difference, tension and pretension in The Forsyte Saga. Its success encouraged Galsworthy to revisit Soames Forsyte in a second trilogy, A Modern Comedy, which follows Soames's obsessive love of his daughter Fleur. In its three volumes, The White Monkey (1924), The Silver Spoon (1936) and Swan Song (1928) he examines the English commercial upper-middle class and its ideologies, its instinct to possess as its only way of distinguishing itself manifested in the poisonous materialism of Soames. Interestingly, this emergent social class which he so vehemently criticises is the very class from which he emerged. He witnessed first-hand its insularity, its chauvinism, its restrictive and oppressive morality, its stubborn imperialism and its materialism, and it is this experience which enables him to write so comfortably about it. Swan Song is widely considered among the best of Galsworthy's writing for the depth of its exploration of society and its heightened emotional subtlety. In 1929 he was appointed to the Order of Merit, despite having turned down a knighthood earlier. He spent his last years writing a third trilogy, End of the Chapter, beginning in 1931 with Maid in Waiting, Flowering Wilderness in 1932 and concluding with Over The River in 1933. These are significantly less coherent works and are indicative of his deteriorating health. Indeed, in 1932 he was awarded the Nobel Prize, though he was too ill to attend the ceremony.

Throughout the course of his career he received honorary degrees from the universities of St Andrews (1922), Manchester (1927), Dublin (1929), Cambridge (1930), Sheffield (1930), Oxford (1931), and Princeton (1931). In 1926 New College, Oxford, elected him as an honourary fellow. In photographs he is portrayed as handsome, fastidiously dressed and dignified. He was unusually compassionate and this saw him involved in several charitable and humane causes throughout the course of his life, including penal reforms, attacks on theatrical censorship and campaigning for animal rights. Though he spent the majority of the final seven years of his life at his home in Bury, West Sussex, it was at his home in

Hampstead, London, that he died of a brain tumour on 31st January, 1933, six weeks after having been too ill to attend the ceremony in honour of his receiving the Nobel Prize. According to demands made in his will he was cremated and his ashes scattered over the South Downs from an aeroplane. Also in his will was his wish to leave cottages to several of his astonished tenants. He is memorialised in Highgate 'New' Cemetery and in the cloisters of New College, Oxford, where he was an honourary fellow.

John Galsworthy – A Concise Bibliography

From the Four Winds, 1897 (as John Sinjohn)
Jocelyn, 1898 (as John Sinjohn)
Villa Rubein, 1900 (as John Sinjohn)
A Man of Devon, 1901 (as John Sinjohn)
The Island Pharisees, 1904
The Silver Box, 1906 (his first play)
The Man of Property, 1906 – First book of The Forsyte Saga (1922)
The Country House, 1907
A Commentary, 1908
Fraternity, 1909
A Justification for the Censorship of Plays, 1909
Strife, 1909
Fraternity, 1909
Joy, 1909
Justice, 1910
A Motley, 1910
The Spirit of Punishment, 1910
Horses in Mines, 1910
The Patrician, 1911
The Little Dream, 1911
The Pigeon, 1912
The Eldest Son, 1912
Quality, 1912
Moods, Songs, and Doggerels, 1912
For Love of Beasts, 1912
The Inn of Tranquillity, 1912
The Dark Flower, 1913
The Fugitive, 1913
The Mob, 1914
The Freelands, 1915
The Little Man, 1915
A Bit o' Love, 1915
A Sheaf, 1916
The Apple Tree, 1916
The Foundations, 1917
Beyond, 1917
Five Tales, 1918
Indian Summer of a Forsyte, 1918 – First interlude of The Forsyte Saga

Saint's Progress, 1919
Addresses in America, 1912
In Chancery, 1920 – Second book of The Forsyte Saga
Awakening, 1920 – Second interlude of The Forsyte Saga
The Skin Game, 1920
To Let, 1921 – Third book of The Forsyte Saga
A Family Man, 1922
The Little Man, 1922
Loyalties, 1922
Windows, 1922
Captures, 1923
Abracadabra, 1924
The Forest, 1924
Old English, 1924
The White Monkey, 1924 – First book of A Modern Comedy (1929)
The Show, 1925
Escape, 1926
The Silver Spoon, 1926 – Second book of A Modern Comedy
Verses New and Old, 1926
Castles in Spain, 1927
A Silent Wooing, 1927 – First Interlude of A Modern Comedy
Passers By, 1927 – Second Interlude of A Modern Comedy
Swan Song, 1928 – Third book of A Modern Comedy
The Manaton Edition, 1923–26 (collection, 30 vols.)
Exiled, 1929
The Roof, 1929
On Forsyte 'Change, 1930
Two Essays on Conrad, 1930
Soames and the Flag, 1930
The Creation of Character in Literature, 1931 (The Romanes Lecture for 1931).
Maid in Waiting, 1931 – First book of End of the Chapter (1934)
Forty Poems, 1932
Flowering Wilderness, 1932 – Second book of End of the Chapter
Autobiographical Letters of Galsworthy: A Correspondence with Frank Harris, 1933
One More River (originally Over the River), 1933 – Third book of End of the Chapter
The Grove Edition, 1927–34 (collection, 27 Vols.)
Collected Poems, 1934
Punch and Go, 1935
The Life and Letters, 1935
The Winter Garden, 1935
Forsytes, Pendyces and Others, 1935
Selected Short Stories, 1935
Glimpses and Reflections, 1937
Galsworthy's Letters to Leon Lion, 1968
Letters from John Galsworthy 1900–1932, 1970
Caravan the assembled tales of John Galsworthy, New York Charles Scribner's Sons 1925

www.ingramcontent.com/pod-product-compliance
Lightning Source LLC
Chambersburg PA
CBHW060146050426
42448CB00010B/2324